MEDIUMSHIP:

OUR HERITAGE

By

Kate Maesen

First Edition 2023

Cover design by Hilary Pitt
Typeset: 2QT Publishing Services
Cover photographs Shutterstock.com

Printed by IngramSpark (UK)

A CIP catalogue record for this book is available
from the British Library
ISBN 978-1-8383594-5-4

Also available as an eBook
ISBN 978-1-8383594-6-1

Dedication

To mediums everywhere – past and present.
Especially those in the Spirit World still working their
profession

Acknowledgements

Profound gratitude goes to James Garfield Tingley and John C Lilek for their ministry in mediumship, whilst on this earth-plane:

To their guides, helpers, inspirers, teachers and loved ones, working alongside and steering them on the pathway of truth.

To Greta Lilek, for the release of manuscripts and cassette recordings relating to the two Reverend's work and in giving her kind permission for their publication.

To Adrian Horn for the Editing and Dr. Mark for the proofreading

To Catherine Cousins and Hilary Pitt of 2QT Publishing Services for the typesetting and cover design.

Contents

Introduction by Kate Maesen 1

Biographies: 3

Part One

Chapter 1 ~

Rev. John Lilek's Presentation Of The

History Of Mediumship 11

Chapter 2 ~

Leading The Way 22

Chapter 3 ~

Casting The Light 35

Chapter 4 ~

Passing On Truths 50

Chapter 5 ~

Sainthood 63

Chapter 6 ~

Light In Every Truth 73

Part Two

Chapter 1 ~

Introduction Of The Reverend

James Garfield Tingley   87

Chapter 2 ~

Let's Go To School   99

Chapter 3 ~

A Religion Of Truth   110

Chapter 4 ~

The Master Medium   129

Chapter 5 ~

The Dead Sea Scrolls   153

Chapter 6 ~

Language   161

Chapter 7 ~

Aquarian Age   169

Chapter 8 ~

A Faith For All Seasons   182

Part Three

Voices Of Worth – Into The Séance Room 207

INTRODUCTION

By Kate Maesen

For many years Mediumship and Spiritualism have been described wrongly as 'the practices used among people who <u>believe</u> that communication occurs between the '<u>dead</u>' and the 'living'.

Mediums, Spiritualists and Spiritualism do not communicate with the '<u>dead</u>' and they are not in need to '<u>believe</u>'. This is because evidential proof has and is still being given from the Spirit World that there is no death only a continuation of life after life.

It is with pleasure that I introduce you to your tutors and inspirers – The Reverends James Garfield Tingley and John C Lilek, who will steer you through the works and workings of mediumship, from its starting point in ancient times and its association with both the Old and New Testaments, concluding with their working practices in the séance room. Their insight into mediumship will add, I'm sure, to your advancement in mediumship. James and John were forward thinking and visionary, and in this book, they cleverly take us back in history and endeavour to reveal truths which have been for many, unknown, overlooked or forgotten. They show us that the past holds the foundations to build on, to fortify and maintain our course of spiritual progression and to be proud of our mediumistic heritage.

It has been my upmost privilege in assembling and presenting for publication parts of the teaching modules of these two exceptional mediums and teachers of Mediumship and Spiritualism and bringing them into the light and circulation for present-day students, or those engaged in mediumship. Although my own mediumistic abilities are longstanding, as I typed out John and James' tutorials, I too have learnt and offer my gratitude to the knowledge gained and imparted by them. By bestowing their work to this earth plane, they have lit a path for many.

Biographies:

John and Greta Lilek taken in their garden in Bucksport Maine USA

Reverend John C Lilek (passed to the higher side of life August 2014)

John C. Lilek was born into the religion of the Russian Orthodox Church and began his Spiritualism pathway in 1986, which opened his door to truth (without the need for faith or a belief system). After first attending tuition by the Reverend Ann Hart, John's own mediumship began to flourish. Always being the student and with an inquisitive and a 'need to know' mind, John delved into the mechanisms of spirit contact and the history behind it. He was taken under the wing of the Reverend James G. Tingley D.D. who over many years, taught, guided and conducted him through the science and spiritual aspects of mediumship, especially physical phenomena.

This work is presented with the intention of 'food for thought' as I'm sure even those at the beginning of their search into mediumistic matters or those embarking on their journey to train as mediums, will find this work of interest if not of value. The intention of combining the works of the two Reverend's is for students to comprehend the beginnings of mediumship and hopefully use parts of John and James's work in their own philosophy addresses.

At this point in time, it is not know precisely where John and James acquired all the information given in their work other than the majority of it came from a range of research as well as their own words. Drawn from folklore, *The Bible*, the *New Testament* and historical sources, it is a compilation of words in order to build teaching modules for students attending their classes at the time. To offer the student a building block for presentations and hopefully, in turn, to encourage the student to formulate their own philosophy techniques when speaking publicly in Spiritualist Churches or Spiritual Centres. As John and James have both now passed to the higher side of life, and are no doubt, still continuing their teachings in tandem, it would be a waste and a shame for their work to gather dust and lie idle, when there are so many students seeking ways to learn and then hopefully progress enough to become mediums and advance to teachers. The aim of these two stalwarts of Spiritualism was to bring back to the fore the art of philosophy and to set its precedence above message giving, which sadly has become too much in demand at the Divine church service, resulting in many ways, to the dilution of the true meaning of Spiritualism, passed down through generations of mediums. The Reverend Sylvia Haynes, Associate Minister in 1968 of the First Spiritual Church USA, firmly believed that the Spiritualist Church erred in "featuring" "messages" to the congregation during the 'worship service' and as a result, outsiders have erroneously regarded Spiritualist churches as gathering places for "fortune tellers".

This work is an exercise in encouraging students to think, to present, build confidence and to understand some of the background of mediumship, from whence it began to emerge and has since been passed verbally, penned and demonstrated, through countless generations.

Before one takes up the controls of driving a vehicle, it is both wise and responsible to first learn the theory before the practical – Here John and James are giving the student the necessary **theory**, before they embark on the **practical** methods of conveying mediumship. K. M.

Rev. John C Lilek's dedication:

"Many of our present day speakers (particularly the student speakers), do not know of Spiritualism's rich heritage. In fact, most do not realize that in its humble beginnings, it is perhaps the oldest religion in the world. We need to go well beyond the Fox Sisters, which as we know, serves more as a breeding ground of scepticism. Even before the time of Jesus, and into history where it all began. Much of this is uncharted territory for the present day Spiritualist. As the predicted prophesies are being fulfilled; more and more 'searchers' for truth will be coming through the doors of the Spiritualist Churches. We need to be ready for them, as well as for our present day congregations. We need to devote more time to our spiritual unfoldment of the mental and physical gifts of mediumship. This is what will keep the churches open and growing, and demonstrate to those who seek the truths of God and Spirit. Todays' Christian churches are now adopting our practices of healing and the message service (which they call prophesies or messages). We need to take it to the next level by bringing in the educational teachings and that most effective tool: **the gift of story-telling** back to the congregation. This in turn will bring forth a more enlightened congregation, as well as future students into our classes. In short we need to reclaim our rich heritage and be proud that we are truly Spiritualists!

I dedicate this work to Spiritualism and its growth, in loving memory of **The Master Teacher** that walked the earth plane; to my teacher and best friend, The Reverend James G. Tingley D.D., now working his calling from the other side. I also owe all that I am and will be to God, my spirit teachers, guides and loved ones that have put me on this path of light. I thank my first teacher and dear friend Rev. Ann L. Hart, whose help and encouragement I am most grateful for.

Good tools make good work. When we call upon the inspiration of God, our work then becomes like that of a chisel – a cut above the rest". J. C. Lilek

MEDIUMSHIP: OUR HERITAGE

PART 1

CHAPTER 1

Rev. John Lilek's presentation of the history of mediumship:

BEGINNINGS

To define Spiritualism's beginnings: we must go to the point in time, when God and the spirit world first made direct contact, beyond the veil to humanity. When men and women acknowledged a higher intelligence and a singular God of all creation as it was there the seeds of spiritualism were planted. To find the truth; we first must seek it out, well beyond the conventional attitudes of thought. The so called 'lost years' of Jesus, are in reality the 'finding years' of Jesus the Christ! For us to even begin to understand this Master Teacher, we must follow in his footsteps through many temples of learning that He attended. To trace recordings of spirit contact whether passed as folklore or written historical facts, beginning with the narratives of Voluspa to modern day times. Mediums of philosophy, religion and science contributed in varying degrees to the moulding of Jesus. As we shall see, contributing to our present day understanding of God and spiritualism:

VOLUSPA: (approximately 6750 years B.C.)

She was the first of God's witnesses officially recorded in the sacred books. As a woman, the name Voluspa means "One who sees the universality of things". "She is considered the mother of religion, by means of her psychic faculty. She has through religion, revealed music, rhythm, song and grammar. She belonged to the Borean race, a white race of wanderers of the North European steppes. A nomadic people who called themselves Kelts, or heroes. Her destiny first became obvious when (at the risk of her own life) she ran and threw herself between two warring chiefs – one her brother and the other her husband. Her voice changed, they held off from fighting because of this supernatural event unfolding. She began to swoon but did not lose consciousness, going into a semi-trance condition. She then heard a loud voice calling her name. She looked up and beside her stood a warrior of colossal stature, encircled by dazzling light. The spirit identified himself as the first Herman, the first hero of their race (he was to the Kelts, what Michael the Archangel was and is to the Christians). He told them to stop the fighting and unite and gave a plan to finally conquer their enemy, which enslaved most of their people. The two chiefs gave an account of what the Great Spirit Herman told them; to rally their troops. Upon their triumphant victory, Voluspa rested at the foot of a large oak tree. Again through her, Herman spoke, told them of their future and concluded his message saying "Respect Teut-tad the Sublime, the Infinite, the Universal Father". Thus Voluspa's powers of clairvoyance and clairaudience revealed the existence of God and the survival of physical death of the human consciousness. Since Voluspa, each tribe had a prophetess. Each would prophesy and divine under the shade of giant oak trees. This is why the oak tree is most sacred and also where our present day philosophies of the "mighty oak" originated.

Voluspa became the model of all the prophetesses, who were known in Europe and Asia. From then on women were elevated to the highest social scale. They became interpreters of Heaven, lawmakers and a college of women was entrusted to regulate all things in religion and government. Each college of women had a Druidess to head it and they uttered the oracles. They were consulted on special affairs and Voluspa on general affairs.

The Druids and even Kings obeyed the Druidesses and all were under the orders of Voluspa. The flute was invented, to imitate the voice of Voluspa and the representation of sounds uttered by her. The Druids developed a system of sounds and rhythms and chants that was taught even to children at an early age. This is how the text of the oracles could be taught very effectively to all people. She was also responsible for systematising speech by means of grammar. The Druids were led by the beauty of Voluspa's speech when giving her oracles. (Messages from Spirit)

~~~
~~~

RAMA: (approximately 6700 years B.C.)

Rama was a priest who took his vocation very seriously. He cultivated his psychic faculties, as well as learned arts, sciences, astrology etc. He was a searcher of deep divine truths and visited other countries obtaining higher secrets to occultism from wise men. Upon returning to his country he was horrified at the extent to which human sacrifice had spread. When plague (elephistisement) broke out amongst the people, he took this as divine chastisement for their sacrilegious practises. He became distressed and as was his custom, lay under the shade of a large oak tree to meditate. He was suddenly awakened by a tall majestic figure, dressed like himself in white robes of the Druids. He was about to ask the meaning of the ring on his finger with the entwined serpent, (perhaps this is the origin of the present day medical symbol), when the stranger took him by the hand, bidding him to arise and led him to a low branch of mistletoe. The spirit then drew from his breast a small golden pruning knife and cut the branch. He murmured a few words on preparing the berry and gave it to Rama and disappeared. The spirit intelligence was later know by the name Aesculapius − (the hope of salvation) and regarded as the Genius of Medicine. Rama prepared the medicine as told and gave it to those suffering the plague who became immediately cured. His fame spread abroad and he was hailed everywhere as a deliverer, the Druids were regarded as divine messengers and Rama as a demi-god. However, jealousy was rising from Voluspa. Though she never insulted or condemned him publicly. Rama's spirit guide had further and more difficult work for him. As the newly elected chief of all priests, he was now told to abolish human sacrifices. Voluspa took every opportunity to express regret for Rama's gentle character. Maliciously softening the first letter of Rama's name, from R to L and transmuting it from Ram to Lam indicative of a contemptible lack of power. Little did they know in time to come, the sacred significance of Lam (Lamb of God) which would be attached to this title!

Rama's power was independent of epithets and he was, Voluspa knew, a dangerous rival. She was determined to offer him the highest honour in her power. And so during a great festival, Voluspa summoned him to the foot of the altar. Rama knew what this meant and declined the honour of submitting his head to the axes of the priests and disobeyed the order. He calculated his only alternatives were to incite civil war or to expatriate himself. At this critical time Rama was granted another wondrous revelation. The spirit that gave him self-confidence by granting him insight into truths beyond the reach of human knowledge appeared once more before him. He told him the Divine Intelligence was satisfied with his work. He was now to spread the Light of Truth upon the earth and the spirit would always be near to help and guide. And it was upon this revelation that Rama founded his life's work – The Spiritualising, The Socialising and the Civilising of the World.

From Persia he conquered India. The war lasted seven years and remarkable phenomena are said to have occurred through the operation of his psychic agency. In deserts when his troops were parched with thirst he, like Moses, caused water to spring from rocks at his command, possibly by means of a divining rod. Again, as with Moses, Heaven-sent manna was produced to appease the hunger of his people. When a different form of epidemic began its devastating course, he received again from his spirit-guide a remedy which arrested its ravages. This time he made use of the juice of a plant called hom.

Everywhere he maintained his authority and prestige amongst his people, priests and monarchs, by means of his occult powers and his so-called miracles. He read thoughts, foresaw the future, he healed the sick, all nature seemed to summit to him. In every word and action of his, there was evidence to all that something was supernormal and then assumed to be supernatural.

Rama become, say the sacred books, the spiritual King of the earth from the North to the South, from the Orient to the Occident. All Asia, Africa and a portion of Europe submitted finally to the civil and religious laws initiated by Rama. He held spiritual sway over Kings of Arabia, Chalea, Siam, Japan, China, Persia, Turania, Caucasus, Plaska and Egypt. Also Ethiopia, Libya, all the colonies in the isles and coasts of the Mediterranean. His colossal wars are, together with great deeds, recounted in the Ramayan Valmiki, said to be the greatest poem in the world. He conquered only to establish, never to destroy. He established on earth a millennium of peace and a government which lasted in its integrity for 3,200 years and was the foundation of all that is best in our civilization today.

In what is called the Council of God, only the holiest

and wisest and best instructed in religion and the arts and sciences were eligible to bring the hierarchy of heaven, and the science of the soul to within the reach of the multitude. Rama instructed the cult of ancestors and thus established a work-a-day connection between Heaven and earth, the living and the mis-called dead. He became – owing to his occult powers and his wisdom obtained by means of his psychic revelations – the spiritual King of all the earth; and there came to him, as there comes to all those possessed of exceptional psychic faculties, the temptation to obtain worldly greatness. He was offered supreme power. Here again his decision was guided by revelation from the spirit world. One day he was meditating under the trees about the offer that had been made to him, Deva Nahousha, his spirit guide appeared. Then, told him that if he accepted the crown, the spirit world, would visit him no more. The choice was to be final. Rama reflected for a moment. He made his great renunciation. The same as Christ later resisted similar temptations of the devil. Rama went to the mountains and there taught his chosen disciples the secrets he had learned, through psychic revelations, concerning this world and the next. It was Rama, in his later years, who fixed the Aryan calendar, and it is to him that we owe the signs of the Zodiac. But whatever remains still to be discovered about the religion initiated by Rama, the basis of his teaching was – One Supreme and Universal Intelligence or God; and the immortality of the soul, reincarnation, the occult of the ancestors and the doctrine of the Eternal Feminine in conjunction with Eternal Masculine.

~~~
~~~

KRISHNA: (approximately 4,000 years B.C.)

The story of Krishna – The founder of Brahmanism, is derived from the story of Vishnou-Pourana and from the Bhagavadgita fragments of the great poem, the Mahabharata – one of the most sacred books of the Brahmans and from other Eastern sources.

The magnificent Empire of Rama, which included, India and the greater part of the known world, after remaining intact in all its glory during the thirty-five centuries, was now (in about the year 3,000 B.C.) in the process of disintegration. During the course of the ages that had elapsed since Rama, sacerdotalism (religious belief as mediators between God and man), had fallen more and more into the hands of men only, and the sacerdotal colleges and the Sovereign Pontiffs were quite willing to admit that in the Deity, the male and female principles were One, provided that this One, was male! They swallowed the female whole and monopolized all the sacerdotal callings, duties and privileges. Irshou who was an out and out feminist, therefore reacted violently to this male aggression and going to the other extreme, demanded priority of place for the female, all along the line from Heaven to hell and to the restoration to women their sacerdotal colleges, their rights to the priesthood and to the pontificate etc. One section of the empire including the Hindus declared that the male element must have control everywhere, in every sphere of life, in Heaven and on earth; whilst the other section known as the Phoenician Shepherds, insisted on similar rights for women. This caused three continents to clash in war and a Universal Empire was thrown into disruption. It was at this time that a great prophet was born, whom the Brahmans (even today) regard as a divine man, one of the most brilliant manifestations of the Divinity – Krishna – the Sacred One, Iezeus the Saviour. Krishna seeing the deplorable conditions, to which the Indian Empire was reduced by rival sections of male and of the female cult, made it his mission to effect a reconciliation of both ideas. This he accomplished by a stroke of genius. He proclaimed that the two faculties, male and female, were equally essential and equally influential; but that they would remain eternally separated and consequently ineffective, if they were not united by a third faculty.

He thus established three principles of the universe, emanating from the Absolute and Ineffable Being – Wodh, whom he regarded as inaccessible to human understanding. He named these Brahma, Vishnu and Siva. This was the origin of the Indian Trinity, which under different names and different emblems has been admitted or known by all the peoples of the earth. Krishna then selected Vishnu as Chief Person of the Trinity whom he thus inspired, reconciled the rival feminine and masculine cults and gave equality of rights to both sexes in all spheres of life. At the same time maintaining the great central truth which has been taught both by Valuspa and Rama – that of one Supreme and Universal Deity.

The similarities between Krishna and the Christ are parallel in many ways and there follow a few examples:

His mother Devaki was a pure and holy Virgin who

in accordance with prophecy had been predestined for the sacred honour. One day she was resting beneath the shade of a giant oak-tree, when she saw a wondrous light; the heavens opened and from this a host of angels, the holiest of holy spirits, of dazzling radiance, overshadowed her and she conceived the child who was to be the son of God, the Saviour of the World – Krishna.

After years of initiation, Krishna seated under the cedars of Mount Meron, began his work of teaching his disciples, Truths, inaccessible to those who are the slaves of the senses. Truths; which he obtained by psychic revelations, namely the immortality of the Soul, the soul's rebirths and its mystic union with God. He taught the triple nature of man – body, soul and spirit. That the Kingdom of Heaven is within us, in short, he taught centuries before the Christian era, the same spiritually inspired truths that later fell from the lips of One (Jesus) whom today millions of people recognize as having had access to Divine Truths. Krishna told of a poor fisherman, who befriended a little starving child. He told the fisherman to cast his net into the Ganges. He did so and the net, on being brought to land, broke under the weight of the fishes. The child – a manifestation of the Divine, disappeared. Krishna further told his disciples that the Son of God (himself) must die, pierced by an arrow in order that the world might believe in him. Soon after this the prophecy was fulfilled and he died, pieced by the arrows of his enemies. The Heavens and the earth were convulsed the moment that he passed. Two faithful women were with him to the end. When his body was burned they threw themselves upon the flames to join their master and the people present say the Son of God, and the two women, did rise from the pyre in a cloud of light.

Krishna's work had a universal value, for his doctrines included two principles of fundamental importance for religion – Namely the doctrine of the immortality of the soul and of progressive existences by reincarnation; and the doctrine corresponding to the idea of the Trinity.

CHAPTER 2

LEADING THE WAY

ORPHEUS (approximately 1,300 Years B.C.)

Orpheus was supposed to have lived about the same time as Moses – that is 1,300 years B.C. and five centuries before Homer. He was possessed of personal charm and beauty as well as of occult gifts. One day while quite young, with the entire world at his feet, he suddenly and unaccountably left Greece. He fled secretly to Samothrace and then to Egypt, where he sought from the priests of Memphis initiation in the sacred occult mysteries. It was the death of his love Eurydice that incited Orpheus to abandon the pleasures of youth. He then pursued the study of psychic science, in order that he might learn how to get in touch with his beloved. He did not suppose that he could master the mysteries of communication between two separate planes by a few sittings with a medium. Nor did he suppose that much good would come to him or to the world at large by interchange of trivialities between himself and his spirit friends.

He became assured of the continued existence of his

Eurydice. He probed to the uttermost depths those mysteries which are beyond the reach of the mere human consciousness. He underwent an initiation of the most severe order, which lasted for twenty years. Only at the end of that time did he consider himself worthy of calling himself an initiate. And of becoming a spiritual guide, capable of helping mankind to some of the wisdom which he had acquired at enormous personal risk and sacrifice. He then returned to Greece and was welcomed by the priests of the Sanctuary of Jupiter as a saviour. His science and enthusiasm transformed their religion, which had been corrupted by the Bacchantes, who were at the height of their degeneracy.

His influences soon reached all the Grecian Temples. By teaching of the sacred mysteries, he formed the religious soul of his country. The religion of Orpheus was coloured by his special sense of the artistic. It was through the love of art that Orpheus, himself a great musician, appealed to his Greek compatriots. His wonderful music was said to have charmed and tamed even the fiercest of animals. His power and popularity were so great that he aroused the jealousy of government. These, after a series of revolutions, forbade the reverencing of his name, burned his books, dispersed his disciples and destroyed his temples. Fortunately, for the cause for which he stood, he died a martyr's death, murdered by Aglaonice, the chief priestess of the Bacchantes. Orpheus will remain for all time, one of the great Initiates of the World.

~~~
~~~

HERMES

Egypt was the great repository of religion and of the occult sciences of antiquity. Within her sacred Temples, safely hidden from the uncultured, were preserved those ancient Mysteries – the life's blood of the religion of the great Initiates. Even when (about 2200 B.C) Egypt was invaded by the Phoenicians and her political independence compromised, the soul of Egypt was kept alive by the Brotherhood of Initiates, (depositories of the ancient science), who safeguarded the occult mysteries from vulgarization, by means of a system of an Initiation of such severity that only the bravest dared to penetrate the inmost recesses of the esoteric doctrines.

When the pendulum of religious thoughts swung from East to West, from Asia into Europe, it was from Egypt that the Prophets of the West – Orpheus and Pythagoras derived their inspiration. Therefore, whether Hermes was historical, legendary or merely a figure representative of Egyptian Initiates, his name (like the word of Buddha of generic origin), must not be omitted. As to Hermes, the Egyptians attributed forty-two books on occult science. From "Vision of Hermes", the centre and summation of Egyptian Initiation and from the figured monuments, as well as from the Jewish and Greek traditions, we can derive some notion of what was meant in those days of Initiation.

For their education, the old Initiates took into account the three-fold nature of man-body, which included intellect; soul – concerned with the psychic faculties and spirit, the Self, which works through soul and body. With these Initiates, science, religion and a philosophy of life were interdependent. To them the attitudes of our scientists would seem childish, which would also include our doctors of medicine, who ignore soul and spirit and also our clergy, who ignore science.

Initiation was a gradual training of the whole human being; Will, Reason and Intuition must all be developed simultaneously. It was believed that by deep study and constant application, man could develop his faculties to incalculable limits and put himself in touch with the occult forces of the Universe. The soul has latent senses and therefore Initiation awakens these. But only 'he' can command 'himself' before he can command others. True Initiation was thus something more than a mere manifestation of psychic force and a performance of conjuring tricks. It involved knowledge of the sciences as were available at the time – the science of minerals and of plants; of history of Man and of people; of medicine, architecture and sacred music. During a long apprenticeship the Initiate must not only know – he must become! None of these old Initiates believed with our modern theologians, that the world was created in six solar days by a caprice of the Almighty. They believed that it was created knowledgeably and gradually, by means of emanation and evolution.

On the completion of an Initiation which lasted sometimes twenty years and included hardships, which few moderns would undergo today, the adept was obliged to swear, under penalty of death, never to reveal the secrets of Osiris, except under the three-fold veil of mythology, symbols and the lesser mysteries.

Mankind today, instead of trying to rediscover the realities for which the ancient symbols stood, prefers to reject the symbols and throw away a priceless heritage of heavenly wisdom. Thus the esoteric (secret) teachings of these Egyptian Mystics and their esoteric monotheism remained within the sacred temples.

<div style="text-align:center">~~~</div>

MOSES (approximately 1,300 B.C.)

It was Moses, the Egyptian Initiate and Priest of Osiris, who brought the principle of Monotheism (belief in one God), out of the esoteric darkness of the temples, into the exoteric (for public) light of history. Moses gave the world at large – through the mediumship of the Hebrew people – the religious truths, which had been jealously guarded secrets of the temples. But who was Moses? He was not a Jew, 'but the natural', as she who found him, would probably have preferred to call him, was the adopted son of the Princess Royal, sister of King Ramses 11. Of a religious temperament and with exceptional psychic faculties, Moses was brought up in the Temple and was deeply initiated in the esoteric sciences of Egypt. This was a fact recognised by amongst others, Philo and by Clement of Alexandra as well as by St. Stephen, who in the Acts of the Apostles, 7th Chapter, 27th verse, reminds his listeners that "Moses was instructed in all the wisdom of the Egyptians and was mighty in his words and works". Indeed without this special training, Moses' work would have been impossible.

The ancients in the days preceding Moses are said to have possessed knowledge, not only of astronomy, astrology, optics, pyrotechnics, acoustics, the compass, music, architecture and anthropology. They also made use of telescopes, microscopes, the telegraph, chemistry, organic and inorganic and chemistry even applied to photography and electricity. They must have had the use of firearms too, as the use of these weapons of destruction was restricted to the Sages of the Temple.

Plato, who himself, was initiated in the sacred mysteries, tells us that a complete civilization existed in Egypt 10,000 years before Menes and the date of Menes was 5,000 years before Christ. Indeed Egypt, by universal acknowledgement, transcended all other lands for its accumulated store of wisdom. The temples were the repositories of this wisdom. Therefore, Moses, who was brought up in the temple, amongst learned priests and Initiates, had at his disposal, all the sciences, secular and sacred, exoteric and esoteric and all the knowledge of the known world.

His library included the Encyclopaedia Abramide of Chaldea, the Hermetic libraries of Egypt and of Ethiopia, the forty-two books on occult science by Hermes relating to the social and divine Synthesis, which were carried in the ceremonies. He had, in fact, according to Menethon, 37,000 volumes dealing with sacred science, including every branch of physical and religious science. Moses was step by step led on and prepared for his great work in the following manner: The priests of Osiris, who committed a murder, were severely judged by the Sacerdotal College — so when

Moses killed the Egyptian who had ill-treated one of the children of Israel, he knew his life hung upon a thread, especially as the King suspected him a rival to the throne. Moses therefore exiled himself and was determined to make expiation for his crime. He fled to Midian, at the head of the Red Sea, where there was a Temple, a sacred centre for the Arabs and the Jews and for men who sought initiation. For centuries this Sanctuary of Sinai and Horeb had been the mystic centre of a monotheistic cult and at this time the High Priest of Midian was one Jethro, a black skinned Ethiopian. (As is well known, Moses married Zipporah, one of Jethro's daughters).

It was under the aegis of Jethro, that Moses underwent voluntarily the horrific psychic ordeal ordained by the priests of Osiris for those who had taken a human life. When he awoke from the cataleptic trance into which, as a final test, he had been plunged, he felt himself a different man. Prior to this he was known as Hosarsiph but now took the name – Moses, which signifies saved.

It was probably in the dark silence of the crypt of Jethro's Temple that Moses heard the voice telling him to go to the Mount of God, to Horeb and Sinai, to the Mount where, from time immemorial, a place had been consecrated to supernormal visions of God and other luminous spirits. Only the bravest and only the highest Initiates dared to venture on that bleak, barren, rocky height to encounter unknown forces. But Moses was brave and he was an Initiate of the highest order and it was probably here, under these circumstances, that he saw the psychic light within the burning bush and heard the voice telling him to lead the children of Israel out of bondage.

It is not necessary to recount the story of Exodus and the methods by which Moses accomplished his great task. Nor is it essential to give examples of his great psychic powers; the story itself is well known, and the psychic aspects have been dealt with. Moses' aim was the organization of an ancient society, a nucleus of people who were the guardians of the sacred truths, which he brought out from the darkness of temples, into the light of universal history. So successfully did he achieve this aim, that it was 1,300 years later from the One! – Greater than Moses – did light the Torch which illuminated the whole world.

~~~

PYTHAGORAS (approximately 582 years B.C.)

Pythagoras lived towards the end of the sixth century B.C. about the same period in which Lao-Tzu was rekindling religious favour in China and when Buddha was preaching on the banks of the Ganges. At this time in Greece the influence of the teaching of Orpheus had waned: the moral and spiritual power of the Temples was annulled. The priests had become politically corrupt and even the sacred mysteries were abused.

It was largely upon the ideas contained in the inspirational wisdom of Orphic fragments, that Pythagoras founded his system of esoteric philosophy. With one voice, the line of their descent was from Orpheus through Pythagoras and Plato. He translated
~~~

the religious thought of his predecessor into intellectual requirements of his day. Pythagoras, though he removed some of the outer casings, which had enshrouded the sacred mysteries, retained those inner veils which could only be lifted by the elect.

Pythagoras was the son of a rich jewel merchant at Samos and the female – Parthenis. His parents must have been of a spiritual and psychic bent of mind, for on their honeymoon, the young couple consulted the Pythoness at Delphi. She foretold that they would have a son who would be useful to the entire world, in all times. She then bade them to go to Ledon in Phoenicia, in order that the predestined son should be born, far away from troubled influences of his country. Thus even before his birth, Pythagoras was dedicated to the gods or spirits.

This child of Parthenis was beautiful, gentle and full of a sense of justice. He had from childhood a deep love of learning and at an early age he used to confer freely with the priests of Samos and with the learned men. But none of this satisfied him. He was always searching, amidst their contradictory teachings, for the Unity of the Great Whole. One night while meditating on these things and gazing into the starry heavens, he had an illumination an enlightenment, in which all the Mystery of the Universe was laid bare. In a flash he saw clearly the Truths, which were inexpressible in human language. To interpret these Truths, he recalled a saying as a child – "The Greeks may possess the science of the gods: it is only in Egypt that can be found the science of God". Therefore after visiting Africa, Asia, Memphis and Babylon and learning all that he could from their wise men, he went to Egypt. There he endured the tests, trials, terrors and ecstasies of an Initiation which lasted twenty years.

He underwent experiences which made it possible for him to realize, not as theory, but as experienced fact, the doctrine of the Logos, of the Universal God and of human evolution.

At every step of the steep ascent, the trials increased in severity. It was necessary even to risk life a hundred times, if he wished to reach the stage of being able safely to handle occult forces. But he was undaunted, for his vision had shown him the life beyond life.

The Egyptian priests soon recognized in Pythagoras, his extraordinary strength of soul and character. They opened for him, all the treasures of their experience and he steeped himself in their lore. From the priests of Memphis, he learned the two magic keys which open all doors of the Universe. They are – the Science of Numbers and the art of Will Power. It was in Egypt that he came to understand the principle of the involution of spirit in matter by universal creation and of its evolution through the development of consciousness.

At the time when Pythagoras was at the point of his returning to Greece, having completed his initiation, Cambyses conquered Egypt and Pythagoras was taken prisoner to Babylon. This apparent calamity was, however, in effect an advantage for him as the Persian wise men had a unique practical knowledge of certain occult arts. They especially understood the handling of psychic or astral lights. At their command, lamps lighted themselves and radiant spirits manifested. The Magi called this incorporeal fire, which they could condense or dissipate at will, the "celestial lion" and the electrical currents of the atmosphere were said to be able to aim as an arrow upon men, they called "serpents". Is it not possible that when the writer of Genesis, tells the story of the rod of Moses, which became a serpent and swallowed up similar 'serpent-rods' of the magicians, he was perhaps referring not to live serpents but to the flames of psychic light, astral light, electrical currents of the atmosphere which in that time were called "serpents of light" which, Moses and the magicians could, like many modern days mediums, produce at will.

Pythagoras is said to have had the gift of healing souls as well as bodies; of talking with animals and even with rivers, the controlling of wild beats by his words and of being in two places at once. He was also able to hear the music and harmony of the spheres of prophesying.

Having been imprisoned for twelve years, Pythagoras returned to Samos after an absence of thirty-four years. He found his country crushed, the schools and temples shut; the wise men and poets had fled before the Persians. But he had the joy of finding, his mother Parthenis, still living, who alone believed he was not dead and that he would return to accomplish his high mission in accordance with the prophecy. Together mother and son fled with their possessions and went into exile to Greece, there to begin his great work – to re-awaken the sleeping gods in the sanctuaries. He went from city to city instructing the priests in the wisdom he had learned in Egypt, Babylon and from the wise men of Chaldea and then he went to Delphi.

He was led to Theoclea, a young girl in the college of the priestesses, who was of a highly refined and spiritual nature. At once they knew that they were the spiritual counterparts of each other. He tested her before everyone in the temple and her mediumship (Clairvoyance and Clairaudience) prevailed. And so Pythagoras poured into the soul of Theoclea the teaching, making her a fitting instrument for divine messages. The temple had now an inspired Pythagoras and priests who were initiated in the divine arts and sciences.

Delphi once more became a Centre of religious life and action. Pythagoras remained there for one year, and it was only after he had instructed the priests in all the sciences of his doctrine and moulded Theoclea for his ministry, that he eventually left Delphi.

At Croton he founded a college for initiates of the laity. Its aim was to make religion "scientific and science" religious. From a study of moral duties and a study of the physical universe, Pythagoras was led to the secret of secrets – the study of the soul. Know yourself and you will know the universe of the gods, the secret of the wise initiates. Women initiates assisted at nocturnal reunions and sometimes priests and priestesses from Delphi and from Eleusis came to confirm the teaching of the Master by giving practical demonstrations of psychic experiences.

At the age of sixty, Pythagoras married. He had two sons and two daughters, who were all worthy of their upbringing. He lived at Croton for thirty years but when reached the age of ninety-years, the reaction against his authority began. An individual named Cylo, who had long nourished hatred against Pythagoras, (because the latter had rejected him as a disciple), stirred up the people against Pythagoras and set fire to the house in which he and forty of his noblest disciples were assembled. With the exception of two – all others were perished.

CHAPTER 3

CASTING THE LIGHT

THE BUDDHA (622–543 B.C.)

The word Buddha is not a proper name. It derives from Budh – Learned, the Enlighted or the Intelligent One. The Buddha's family name was Gautama, his individual name was Saddharta. He was born about the middle of the fifth century B.C. of royal parentage, in Central India. He was therefore contemporary with Pythagoras and with Lao-Tzu. Thus in three widely different portions of the globe, the lamp-lighters of God were lighting simultaneously their inextinguishable lamps.

Before his birth, the Brahmans had predicted that he would become a holy man and would wander in poverty and want. His parents therefore took every precaution to prevent the fulfilment of this prophesy. They married him to a beautiful and charming Princess and surrounded him with every luxury, but all in vain. The young Prince was always meditating how he could redeem mankind from ignorance and from the suffering that comes from ignorance.

He was granted three successive visions of angels,

which appeared under the guise respectively of old age, of disease and of death. These caused him to meditate more earnestly on how he could reduce the suffering of the world. When the appropriate moment had arrived, another vision was to disclose. A spirit appeared to him, that the time had now come for him to reveal himself to the world. He was now to set forth upon his mission.

From that moment, all the desperate attempts of his relations to keep him from his purpose were unveiling. One night he evaded the guards sent by the King to prevent his departure, took a last long look at the young wife sleeping with her hand upon the head of their new-born babe (the much-prized heir to the kingdom) and with his favourite charioteer (named Chondaka) he escaped from the bondage of domestic happiness and of princely luxury.

So at the age of twenty-nine years, this young Prince, world-renowned for his beauty of person as well as for his wisdom, inspired from the spirit-world, abandoned wife, child, palaces and earthly pleasure and set forth to seek and help others find the secret of the Universe. He first learned all that the Brahmans could teach him, but he remained unsatisfied. He then underwent years of rigorous self-mortification (severe discipline, humiliation) and asceticism (training by exercise). It was during this time that Mara, the great tempter and evil spirit, appeared to him and urged him to desist from his mission and promised him all the Kingdoms of the world and the glory of them, if he would give up his enterprise.

However, he continued his visions and his ecstasies, until at last one day, while seated in semi-trance, under the shade of a large fig-tree, subsequently called the Tree of Wisdom, he had a glorious and convincing vision. The Archangel Brahma came and ministered to him and he attained what he knew was perfect wisdom.

Buddha preached Love and Universal Charity as the key to spiritual wisdom, freedom and enlightenment and did not advocate a torturing self-mortification. The mind must be purified from sensuousness, evil passions and unholy desires but these moral evils would not be eliminated by torturing the body. The great essential was change of heart.

Like all Great Ones he was lacking self-confidence of his powers but he finally overcame his scruples by the argument that one-third of mankind is in error and will remain in error; one-third has the truth and will keep the truth; but one-third is uncertain and it is these, who he might save. Therefore, with overwhelming pity for the number being plunged in uncertainty, he determined to overcome his lack of confidence. He fixed the basis of his doctrine, with the intention of opening for mankind "the gates of immortality".

We must refer briefly to the doctrine generally misunderstood, the doctrine of Nirvana. When Buddha promised to the faithful cessation of existence after this life, he means cessation from the dreary round of earthly reincarnations, in which, as he believed, man is otherwise involved. He does not mean annihilation, as is so often supposed. As how could he speak of immortality if he had annihilation in his mind? For example, when he stated on his mission, after that night under the Tree of Wisdom, meeting an acquaintance struck with his appearance, who asked him what religion it was that made him so glad, and yet so calm, and where was he going? He replied "I am now going to the city of Benares, to establish the Kingdom of Righteousness, to give light to those enshrouded in darkness and to open the gate of immortality to men".

As his last hour approached, the Buddha summoned his disciples and after a moment's silent meditation he addressed himself to Ananda – his relative as well as his favourite disciple. He said "When I shall have disappeared from the state of existence and be no longer with you, do not believe that the Buddha has left you, and ceased to dwell among you. Do not think, therefore, nor believe, that the Buddha has disappeared and is no more with you".

It is also clearly stated that Gautama (Buddha) told his disciples that he had already entered Nirvana, while yet in the body. In alluring to a stage still in the flesh, the Buddha is reported to have said, "He is indeed blest, having conquered all the passions and attained the stage of Nirvana. He said "Many have reached Nirvana even in this life". Clearly therefore, reaching Nirvana meant for the Buddha what gaining the Kingdom of Heaven meant to the Christ.

LAO-TZU (604 B.C.)

It is impossible to discuss Lao-Tzu the great Chinese mystic philosopher, without including both Chuang-Tzu, a celebrated disciple who lived three centuries later than his revered master and Confucius. For Chuang-Tzu was to Lao-Tzu, what Plato was to Socrates, and what Paul was to Christianity. It was in a large measure due to his desire to refute the materialism of Confucius, that Chuang-Tzu wrote, extolling in his brilliant dialogues, the transcendental teaching of Lao-Tzu.

Indeed these three names form a Chinese triangle of which Chuang-Tzu is the apex and Lao-Tzu and Confucius are the two basic points. (He was called Lao-Tzu, which means "Old Boy", because at his birth he had the appearance of an old man with grey hair). It is more than probable that but for the immortality ensured to Lao-Tzu by the brilliant literary gift of Chuang-Tzu, the precious collections of Lao-Tzu's sayings in the Tao-The-King would never have passed the Chinese wall. They would have been submerged beneath the flood of Confucianism, which was fashionable in China in the fourth century.

Lao-Tzu was imperial historiographer, the keeper of the royal archives. He thus had easy access to the literature of the Western World and probably would have known something of the philosophy of Pythagoras, his contemporary.

Lao-Tzu rejected any set system of teaching, declaring "Those who knew did not speak, while those who spoke did not know". He taught the same Truths that have been revealed by his great predecessors and by his great successors in all time, namely; the Immanence of the Eternal Principle in all that it is. It means the soul is an emanation from the Divine, and that life is perfect in proportion as it becomes one with that from which it came and loses what is individual in it. The true sage takes his refuge in God and learns that there is no distinction between subject and object. "This is the very axis of Tao" (God), that we must use the light that is within us to revert to our natural clearness of sight, the relativity of all human perception and (2,500 years before Einstein) – the relativity even of space and time.

He also taught that we must return good for evil; that the greatest conquest is that of self. That he who is strong must become weak. That he who would be first must be last. That goodness of doing good is not real good. He also taught that we may look forward to another and a higher life, that the perfect man is a spiritual being.

Lao-Tzu differentiates the "human intellect from the Intelligence that is of God", asserting that "man's intellect, however keen, can never reach the root". "The soul" he said, "is immortal and divine; life and death are all-powerful but cannot affect it". To know this constitutes the sage. I will lead you "he says", through the portals of Eternity, into the domain of Infinity. My light is the light of sun and moon. My life is the life of heaven and earth. I know not who comes and who goes. Men say all die, but I endure for ever". This is that place he found, Tao (God).

Confucius had a deep respect for this great Master Teacher Lao-Tzu and visited him on many occasions, learning more each time. On his first meeting, Lao-Tzu after listening to his philosophy, rebuked him for his ostentatious way of travelling, his love of princes, of publicity and of popularity. "Put away Sir, "he said", "your haughty airs and many desires, your flashy manner and extravagant will; these are all unprofitable to you. "This is all I have to say to you". Confucius did not take offense and came back again and again, a humbler, wiser man.

The idea of the Tao (God) alone brings Lao-Tzu into the line with all the other Torchbearers. It enables us to clearly visualize this old Chinese Mystic as one who drew his wisdom at first hand and from the fountain's head.

HERACLITUS (535 B.C.)

Through Heraclitus, his doctrine of the Logos, which in a tangible and recognisable manner, linked ancient Greek religious thought, which itself was linked as we have seen with ancient Egyptian, Persian, Chaldean and Aryan thought, with Christianity, through Plato, Philo, St John and Justin Martyr. Heraclitus believed that he had a prophetic vocation. This probably accounts for the symbolic and difficult language in which he clothed his message, "The Lord, "he said, whose is the oracle at Delphi, neither utters nor yet conceals his meaning". Even Socrates had some difficulty in understanding him, for Adam tells us Euripides once lent Socrates a copy of Heraclitus's book and when Adam asked what he thought of it, Socrates replied, "The parts I understood are splendid; and I suppose what I fail to understand were splendid too; only I would need a Delian diver to fathom it".

We are told by Diogenes Laertius that in his youth, Heraclitus professed to know nothing, but declared himself, omniscient after he became a man, which seems to indicate that he attained wisdom, like many teachers, by means of illumination from the higher plane, by means of revelation which mere worldly research was powerless to bestow. The main feature of this illumination was expressed in the idea of what he calls the Logos.

The characteristic of this Logos (signs) of Heraclitus were: It was to be experienced: it was universal; it was dive (descent) and it was eternal. The Logos speaks through man, but is sometimes apart from his own intellect. It is all-knowing, is the knowledge by which all things are steered through. The duty of man is to obey this Logos, but most men said Heraclitus neither see nor hear it. The Logos, Heraclitus said it is always existent, but man fails to understand it both before they have heard it and when they have heard it. It is something which reveals itself in other ways than through the spoken word.

Heraclitus begins his book with the sentence, "Having hearkened not unto me, but to the Logos". This means that it is not to his voice that he bids them give heed, but to the inspired word, that is to the Logos – The divine spirit, which speaks through him; and we are inevitably reminded of the words of Christ, "Not I, but the Father who dwelleth in me". It was this Logos, which spoke through Jesus to such effect that to Philo, to St John and to the Fathers of the Church, Jesus became the Logos (the sign) Incarnate. So in this definite manner, it was by means of this common knowledge of the phenomenon of spirit inspiration, that the historical continuity of the doctrine of the Logos was insured from Heraclitus through Plato, Philo, the Alexandrine school, to St John and Justin Martyr.

SOCRATES (470–399 B.C.)

Socrates is an essential link in the chain of Great Initiates as he bridged the gulf between the two worlds of religious thought – the prehistoric and the historic – the ancient and the modern – between the religious philosophy of Pythagoras and the intellectual religion of Plato. It was through the teaching of Socrates that Plato was led to study those ancient esoteric and Pythagorean truths which shine through the Platonic philosophy.

Socrates was born near Athens of poor parents, about the year 470 B.C. His father was a worker in stone and Socrates himself started life as a sculptor. He gave up moulding stone into images of men to mould souls into images of God. "The world", he said, "could do without statues but it could not do without God".

Socrates was the inspiration of Plato and of Erasmus who in the sixteenth century, called him – one of the great saints of religion. Men said of Socrates that he was not merely a man but an historical movement. All of Socrates teachings were directed at "Know Thyself" – the motto over the portico of the Delphic Temple and was the starting point and the goal for all his famous cross-examinations. *"Cast your character into the crucible of self-examination and when you have discarded the dross take what is left, if any, it has the properties of clay and with your own will, mould it after the pattern, not the temporal but of eternal things."*

When Chaerephon asked the Oracle at Delphi if there were any wiser than Socrates, she replied there was none wiser than he. Socrates realized that this meant that he alone was wise because he alone knew how ignorant he was of the only knowledge which could be of service to the soul.

Socrates describes "the Voice", which accompanied him and which intervened in all the affairs of his life by saying: "You have often heard me say, that a sort of divine thing, a spirit agency, comes into my experience. Ever since boyhood, I have had experiences of a certain Voice which, when it comes to me, always forbids me to do something which I am going to do, but which never commands me to do anything; it is this which opposes my following a political career".

According to Plato, the divine sign, (the Voice), performed also the useful function of indicating to Socrates, whom he should refuse. It was in obedience to the dictates of this voice that he refrained from preparing any set defence when on trial.

Xenophon said that Socrates claimed never to have been deceived by the voice and never misled friends by any advice he gave upon the strength of it. "Although I have reported to numbers of friends the counsels of Heaven, I have never at any time been shown to be a deceiver or deceived". Without doubt Socrates put implicit faith in his divine sign, as he called it, and rendered it unquestioning obedience.

Socrates was also in the habit of going into trance and this was recorded in many instances. He declared that discussions with 'others' while in trance "was a duty imposed upon him by gods and that he was confirmed in it by oracles, visions and in every way in which the will of the divine power was ever signified to anyone".

Socrates was a convinced believer in the Orphic-Pythagorean doctrine of the soul, according to which, this present life in the body is only the prelude to more real and endless life to come after the separation of the soul and body. The chief duty of man is to live for this redemption of the soul by means of "philosophy". And that he himself had been initiated in the Mysteries of the Pythagorean cult is the more probable from the inspired words which flow from his lips during his last hour on earth. He is talking to his chosen disciples on the soul and immortality and he says; "And I fancy that the men who established our Mysteries and had a very real meaning; in truth they have been telling us in parables all the time that whosoever cometh to Hades (underworlds) uninitiated and profane, will lie in the mire; while he that has been purified and initiated shall dwell with the gods. For as they say in the Mysteries;

the thyrsus-bearers are many, but the inspired are few,
(Many are called, but few are chosen). And by these
last I believe are meant only the true philosophers. I
in my life have striven as hard as I was able and have
left nothing undone that I might become one of them.
Whether I have striven in the right way and whether I
have succeeded or not, I suppose that I shall learn in a
little while, when I reach the other world, if it be the
will of God".

PLATO (429 B.C.)

Plato had been initiated into the Mysteries of esoteric
wisdom and was, like Socrates, a follower of Pythagoras
and possessed an intimate knowledge of psychic truths.
For to Plato, science and religion were inseparable, in
as much as he could not conceive that man could desire
knowledge except for the attainment of that which he
believed or could alone be known – the unseen, the
eternal, the divine. For of the seen and temporal, there
is no knowledge, there can only be opinion.

Plato was born about the year 429 B.C. and was therefore
contemporary with Socrates. It was at the age of twenty-
seven years, at a moment when Plato was on the point
of producing a tragedy he had composed, that he first
came in touch with Socrates who was disputing with
his disciples in the gardens of Academy. This interview
revolutionized Plato's life. It caused him to divert the
main stream of his great intellect from dramatic and
poetic to philosophical and religious channels. It almost
seems as if he, Socrates, must have had forewarning of

its importance. It is related by Diogenes Laertius that on the night before this meeting with Plato, Socrates dreamed that a young swan rested for a moment on his knees. Then the swan suddenly grew wings and flew aloft, uttering a sweet cry – an excellent illustration of the relationship which was to exist between Plato and his beloved master Socrates.

Plato's real Initiation began when he had seen his friend and teacher Socrates during his last hours on earth, conversing calmly with his disciples on immortality and the sacred mysteries. Life in Athens would now be unbearable without his beloved master. Plato having received the great impulsion then set himself, as all the great predecessors of Socrates had done, to gain wisdom from other lands. He was initiated in the mysteries of Eleusis. He followed the teachings of various philosophers in Asia Minor. Then he went, of course to Egypt, to get in touch with learned priests and the psychic sages. He went through the initiation of Isis. He did not, like Pythagoras, reach the highest stage of adept. He stopped short of the third degree, which gives intellectual clarity.

He then went to Italy, to familiarise himself with the Pythagoreans. He bought, for an enormous sum, a Manuscript of the Master. Having thus traced the esoteric traditions of Pythagoras to the very fountain-head, he borrowed from this philosopher the main ideas and the framework of his own system of philosophy.

Plato was above all things practical and having satisfied himself as to the source and the goal of all wisdom, he set to work to spread his knowledge. He followed the example of Pythagoras, he founded his famous Academy, which lasted a century and was prolonged into the great school of Alexandria. It was the model of the universities and schools of philosophy that have since risen.

The keynote and spirit of Plato's teaching was to mature and develop the germ of personality rather than to impress it from without. According to Plato, the cramming of uncorrelated facts, the method attributed by him to some of the professional teachers of his day, was a travesty of true education. This travesty from which, we are scarcely even beginning to emerge from today.

Plato's main thesis that "the ultimate aim of education is to raise the soul out of temporal and visible, into the sphere of that invisible and Eternal Being to which she, by rights, belongs". He throughout implies a continuous growth in knowledge through successive lives, with immortality as the crown and consummation of all knowledge.

The influence of Plato's idea of the World-soul as "made in the image of God" and as, "the only-begotten of the Father", the relationship being conceived as that of father and son, is clearly traceable in Christian theology. Plato's famous <u>Theory of Ideas</u> was expressing in his own poetic, dramatic and inimitable language, not only the tenets of his spiritual predecessors, but the present-day belief of spiritualists. He can only be understood by those who believe in the reality of the world of spirit. It was Plato's belief in the existence of spirit which gave force to his doctrine that the true, the imperishable realities are the things which are to the majority – "Unseen".

49

CHAPTER 4

PASSING ON TRUTHS

THE CHRIST

As we look to Jesus as the most important and most identified in the sequences of mediums, we will focus on who He is in relation to our mediumship, religion, philosophy and science. To even attempt to bring into the light his Conception, Resurrection and Ascension would bring numerous arguments by many of our present day religions. Even theories presented by the disciples Matthew and Luke differ. We will therefore, focus more on who Jesus was, his studies and how religion perceives him and how Spiritualists sees the "Son of God". A great deal might be said also concerning the words, "Son of God", as used in the New Testament. Paul's understanding of this phrase certainly does not imply any sense of the exclusive 'son' connection of Jesus to the Father of All. For in Romans 8:14, he says "For as many as are laid by the Spirit of God, these are the sons of God". There is also another sense in which the name Son of God was often used. In the days when there were four degrees of Initiation into the Sacred Mysteries, that those who attained the second degree

were called the Sons of Man, and that it was reserved
for those who reached the fourth and highest degree,
to be called the Sons of God. And in this respect the
Christ was doubtless recognized to be, as he truthfully
was, the Son of God in a sense that was unique.

There were days when it was taken for granted that
men could not expect to understand things pertaining
to the Spirit. Man's understanding, while on earth, was
supposed to be finite and incapable of comprehending
the Infinite. He must therefore leave the Infinite
alone and be content with any sentimental course the
Churches might impose upon them – That man has a
dual nature in that he is man now and spirit henceforth;
but that he is both Man and Spirit here and now, was
completely ignored. It was therefore, also ignored that
as Spirit, man might, if he attuned himself to spiritual
conditions, gain some understanding, or at least some
inkling, of spiritual realities.

Today, for many thousands of intellectual people, the
word spirit is not far away from metaphysical abstraction
and beyond the comprehension of mundane minds.
Spiritualists know today from personal experiences that
Spirit is a concrete reality, which can be scientifically
studied in laboratories. It is perhaps natural that when
difference in degree is great, men are apt to drift into
assuming differences in kind. In some classes of animal
life it is true that excessive differences in degree may
lead to a new type. If God is Divine by virtue of being
Spirit – and we only know of Him as Spirit – then it was
by virtue of being Spirit that Jesus was Divine and it is
by virtue of this same, that Man is Divine.

Man's recognition of his power of functioning as a Spirit, as well as of his power of functioning as a Man, can only be regained through exercising his psychic faculties – those faculties through which alone Spirit is able to function on this earth. For as the body functions by means of the physical, and the mind by means of the intellectual faculties, so it is by means of the physical faculties that the soul of Man can function.

Readers who will take the trouble to compare the main events in the life of Jesus – the world's greatest and noblest bearer of the Torch of Truth, with the events which have been recorded in the lives of the lesser Truth bearers, will have no difficulty in realising that the basic features of the Christian Religion, (those events which have been regarded by the Churches as affording evidence, in the Christ i.e. of a nature that was supernatural and unique), will see that the events are closely paralleled in the lives of the mediums already written and named. Students of psychic science will also observe that these occurrences are in conformity with phenomena which are taking place today. This can be verified by our scientific researchers; they belong therefore to a category which is neither supernatural nor unique. The Christ's works of healing were conducted upon lines which are well understood and which are successfully practiced today. The Transfiguration, the so-called Resurrection, the post-resurrection appearances, and the Ascension, though all on a scale of sublimity that has never been equalled, present no features which are unfamiliar to modern students of psychic science. These events were neither supernatural nor unique. They were of a nature which entitles us to look with human pride and gratitude to Jesus as an example of what could be achieved by life-long training and self-sacrifice and by a rare balanced combination of psychic, spiritual and moral qualities.

Also in pursuance of one of our main arguments, is it not true of Jesus, as is of the lesser Truth bearers in this series, that but for events in His life which partook of a supernormal, but not supernatural, we should never have known of the Saviour. But for His signs and wonders, His so-called miracles and His works of healing, the multitude would have paid no heed to His preaching. And by His mis-name Resurrection, His post-resurrection appearances and His Ascension, Christianity would have died upon the Cross.

If today's Churches would, for instance make themselves acquainted with the modus operandi of those metaphysical laws in accordance with which Christ's Transfiguration, Resurrection and Ascension were affected, they would be able to bring the truth of these events home to the heart and understanding both of the learned and of the simple: they would speak from conviction and therefore with power, and religion would be revolutionized. If they would take the trouble to discover – and they are discoverable – the methods by which Christ and His disciples healed the sick and exorcised evil, they would have no cause to complain of empty churches. The healing of the sick bodies and the restoration to spiritual health of sick souls are, as Christ knew, processes which are interdependent. They are affected not by means of asserting faith in supernatural myths, but are the attainment of a simple and spiritual wisdom which is obtained from the one and only source of wisdom.

There is no reason to believe that Jesus spent those years of His early life before His ministry, years of which in the Gospel we have no record, serving a long period of initiation in the Sacred Mysteries, with the Order of the Essenians. They were an ascetic sect who, scattered in groups over Palestine and Egypt. They were the last of the Brotherhood of the Prophets organized by Samuel.

It was doubtless from the Essenians, whose chief public mission was the healing of the physical and of moral sickness by methods of which they had made a special study, that Jesus learned the secrets of His great healing power. From their custom of communal repasts that He derived His Sacramental Supper; from their Cup of final Initiation, which contained "the wine of the true vine of the Lord", His Communion Cup of the last Supper. It was therefore probably in common with the Essenians, that Jesus practiced celibacy, community of goods, free hospitality to brethren of the order; that He taught love of neighbour, humility, prohibition to take the oath and that he wore linen garments.

From the Essenians it was, in short, that he derived much of that esoteric wisdom that they had inherited in direct line from Pythagoras, from Orpheus and from Krishna. It was with these exemplary moral and occultly learned Essenians that He initiated and that He then attained both to the second degree and became as He called Himself a "Son of Man" and also to the highest degree and became a "Son of God".

Therefore in acknowledging Christ, we are more than Christians, we are the followers of Plato, Pythagoras and of Rama. But we hindered from seeing this, we are hindered from realizing the vastness, the age long character of our religious heritage. The Churches in accentuating the Divinity of Christ have estranged us from a consciousness of the Divinity inherent in every man who is "in the image of God".

We, however, know today that though one planet differs from another, this is in magnitude only and not in kind. They are all linked as interdependent units in gravitation Whole, in obedience to the same great Central Sun. And as the study of the Heavens became a stimulating science when the more comprehensive knowledge of Copernicus replaced the old belief that the sun and all the universe revolved around the Earth, so will the study of Religion become a glorious and absorbing science, when men realize the Revelation has not been restricted within the narrow orbit prescribed by the doctrines of the Church, but that Revelation is the Breath of God, broadcasted through the Universe in accents, which can be understood by all those who, like the Great Initiates, attune their souls to catch sounds from the Divine.

APOLLONIUS of TYANA (A.D. 20)

The great psychic philosopher of the Greek city of Tyana in Cappadocia is of a special interest as he was contemporary with Jesus, but for this very reason he is little known, as the Christians, began to base their claim to the divinity of the Christ upon His supernormal wonders, were unwilling to admit that similar wonders could be worked by anyone else. Hierocles, a provincial governor under the Emperor Diocletian, had drawn a parallel between Apollonius and Jesus, and had tried to show that Apollonius had been a great sage, as holy a man and as wonderful in working miracles and in exorcising demons, as Jesus.

Apollonius was born about the year A.D. 20. He belonged to a wealthy and well-connected family, and besides having exceptional abilities and a great psychic faculty, he was possessed of remarkable personal beauty. At the age of fourteen years, he devoted himself to trying to discover, amongst the numerous Greek philosophies, some school of thought which would enable him to live up to his ideals. At the age of sixteen he definitely, "soared into the Pythagorean life".

However, Apollonius was not a Pythagorean in theory only. He put his principles into practice. His food was fruit and vegetables. He abstained from wine, though it was a clean drink, it endangered the mental balance and system and darkened as with mud, the ether which is in the soul. He went barefoot; let his hair grow long; declining to wear any animal product and wore only linen garments.

Marvellous cures are attributed to Apollonius, for like his great master Pythagoras, he considered healing, the most important of the divine arts. Under his guidance, the temple became a centre for philosophy and for the science of religion – The understanding of spiritual truths which were the base of the esoteric mysteries.

On coming of age he distributed the fortune he had inherited from his father amongst his relatives, retaining for himself a bare pittance. Then he took, as Pythagoras had done, the vow of silence for five years. Then he journeyed from city to city and from temple to temple instructing the priests and the various communities and brotherhoods and all those who were endeavouring to lead the inner life.

Before Apollonius considered himself possessed of the wisdom essential to be a Sage and true Initiate, he followed the example of the great Teachers and he travelled extensively. He wondered on foot over Assyria, Persia, Egypt and India, conversing with and learning wisdom from the Magi of Persia, the ascetics of Egypt and above all from the Brahmans of India. Apollonius was made marvel at the feats of levitation and at the great power of foresight. These Sages not only knew by psychic means the history of Apollonius in his present life, but they also were able to discuss with him the events of a previous incarnation when he had, as he remembered, been a pilot (navigator) on an Egyptian vessel.

Philostratus informs us, for example, that one day Apollonius asked the Sages of what they thought the cosmos was composed? – Of the four elements? – Not four answered Larchus but five. When Apollonius further asked, how can there be a fifth alongside of water, air, earth and fire? Larchus answered in words which could be of interest to the readers of Sir Oliver Lodge (who made a profound study of the ether, its functions and its uses) "There is, said the Indian Sage, "the ether, which we must regard as 'the stuff of the gods' (spirits) are made; for just as all mortal creatures inhale the air, so immortal and divine natures inhale the ether". Philostratus in estimating the psychic attainments of his hero (Apollonius) tells us that he knew all the languages without ever having leaned them. This probably means that in trance he could, as many mediums can, speak and understand foreign tongues. He also understood, it is said, the language of birds and of animals. He could read most thoughts of man and of course heal bodily sickness and exorcise demons.

He is reputed to have raised from the dead, a young girl, daughter of one of the Consuls of Rome, who had died in the hour of her marriage. He stopped the funeral procession and saying to the lamenting bridegroom, "I will stay the tears you are shedding for the maiden". He approached the bier and making some passes over the body of the girl, whispered in her ear; and at once she awoke from her seeming death and spoke and returned in health to her father's house. For according to occult belief, so long as the (silver) cord, which unites the astral with the physical body, has not yet been severed, restoration to life is feasible.

Philostratus makes a fascinating story of an account which Apollonius gives of a séance at which the spirit of Achilles had appeared to him. Apollonius, together with Damis and friends, were voyaging along the coast of Euboes. The sea was very calm and all the company, except Damis, were contentedly conversing on general subjects. Damis however, seemed grumpy and disagreeable. Apollonius saw something in his mind and asked him, since he could not possibly be sea-sick on such a calm sea, what was the matter. Damis complained that Apollonius knew how eager they all were to hear about the séance at which the spirit of Achilles had appeared and yet he, Apollonius, kept putting them off with small talk about the scenery through which they were passing. "All right then said Apollonius, if you won't accuse me of bragging, I'll tell you all about it".

> There upon a slight earthquake shook the neighbourhood and Achilles appeared. Apollonius asked him five questions and to all of these the spirit hero replied informatively. He then vanished with a flame of summer lightning. 'An admirable description of the psychic light that often accompanies materialization at séances'.

Of his many gifts, Apollonius had the ability to literally vanish out of sight, even before large groups of people and reappear miles away. One of the stories begins with – he was living in Crete, where he had become a great centre of admiration, with the people insisting in spite of his protests, that he was divine. He came late one night to the temple, which was guarded by fierce dogs. These, however, instead of barking at his approach, fawned upon him, where the guards arrested him as a wizard and placed him in bonds. About midnight Apollonius loosened his bonds and ran to the doors of the temple, which opened to receive him. When he had passed through; the doors closed of their own accord and there were heard by the prison authorities who had followed Apollonius, a chorus of maidens singing from within the temple. "Hasten thou from earth, hasten thou to heaven, hasten!" and Apollonius was seen no more.

The passing of Apollonius at the age of about eighty years was also characteristic of Moses and other prophets and no one knows where his sepulchre is to this day.

PLOTINUS (A.D.204)

Plotinus is both for Spiritualists and for the Christians today an interesting and instructive figure. For not only was he, as is universally admitted, the noblest representative of Neoplatonism, but this school of religious thought for which he stood was the consummation of the best religious philosophy of the old Initiates. Its aim and ethics were the highest and the purest to which man could aspire.

The teachings of Plotinus concern the soul, the spirit and things pertaining to religion and revelations were based on his own personal experiences of the reality of the super-sensual world. Thus his teaching carried with it weight of unimpeachable authority. Plotinus, in short, was an Initiate and was possessed of considerable psychic power. He is supposed to have been born in Egypt but he was so ashamed of having to be reborn on this earth that he always refused to disclose details of such a degrading event. From early youth he determined to devote his life to the search for truth. After receiving a liberal education in Alexandria, he went to Persia and to India, there to get in touch with occult learning of the Magi and the Brahmans. Then returning to Alexandria, he sought wisdom from one after another of the renowned teachers of that city, which was celebrated for its schools of philosophy. But he sought in vain, until one day, when he was twenty-eight years of age and had given up hope of finding what he needed, he was persuaded to go and hear a certain Ammonius Saccus, and directly Ammonius began to speak, Plotinus exclaimed, "This is the man I was looking for".

Ammonius was well versed in occult mysteries and it was doubtless this aspect of his teaching which appealed to Plotinus and which provided him with that which he had been unable to find elsewhere in Alexandria. Plotinus studied with Ammonius and he learned the value for purposes of revelation, of that state of super-consciousness which is corresponding to our modern trance and which was then described as ecstasy and which is a condition of the fourth-dimensional consciousness, especially favourable for the reception of spiritual truths.

The state of ecstasy to which Plotinus was able to attain, as "a state of the soul which transforms it in such a way that it then perceives what was previously hidden", we today refer to as trance, but both trance and ecstasy denote the suspension of normal consciousness and the soul's flight to another fourth-dimensional plane.

There is indeed plenty of evidence to show that Plotinus was an Initiate, that he was possessed of the psychic faculty and that he used this not merely to obtain news of departed friends, but to get in touch with the Divine. In this sense Plotinus was indeed a great mystic philosopher and when he spoke of the demonstrability of an Ideal Universe, (a model of the phenomenal world with which we are acquainted), and when he tells us of an Order of Beings of ethereal essence, he speaks thus because he has himself been born into that super-sensual, that "Ideal World", and can no more doubt of its existence, or doubt that it is inhabited by beings of a non-corporeal type.

CHAPTER 5

SAINTHOOD

JOAN OF ARC (A.D.1412)

In all history, sacred or secular, there is probably no story which better illustrates the influence of the psychic faculty on those who have been leaders of men, than the story of the Maid of Orleans. The story in a sense is well known, but amongst the general public it has never been appreciatively understood, mainly because the psychic gifts which enabled Joan to carry out her work have not been understood. The divine source, of her inspiration was never for a moment in doubt.

"I come," she proclaimed, "everywhere, from the King of Heaven, and I will bring you the help of Heaven." And she did. Joan, who is described by Conan Doyle as the most spiritual being next to the Christ (Preface to the Mystery of Joan of Arc, by Leon Denis, translated by A. Conan Doyle) was born of poor parents, in the village of Domremy in the East of France, in the year 1412, during times that were full of misery for her country. There were no League of Nations to interfere and the English King, Henry V, on pretext of having married the French Princess Katherine, was engaged in the talk of "conquering France". The French themselves were curiously enough divided in their sympathies, mainly owing to the indolence, imbecility and indecision of the Dauphin Charles, and throughout the country plunder, rapine and confusion were rampant.

Joan was not merely a sentimental dreamer; she must have been a normally healthy and athletic child. One day she and some other girls and boys in her village were running a race for a garland of flowers and she was easily the winner. For psychic students this race has a special interest, for as Joan was running, another child who was looking on cried out, "Joan, I see you flying along without touching the ground". Was this perhaps the "pressure upon her", of the driving force that is behind evolution, or was it not quite simply a form of levitation (**similar to that which on a certain occasion, as we shall read later, confused and upset St Teresa during a service in the choir of a church**). After the race, Joan seemed to be in trance and she heard a voice which told her to go home as her mother needed her. Another day about midday she was standing in her father's garden, when she saw a bright light like a shining cloud, as she described it, and an angelic figure, a spirit voice spoke and told her to be a good girl and go to church and go to save France. Though she was at first afraid, she replied quite sensibly that she was only a poor girl who could not ride or lead the soldiers into war. However, the voice kept on telling her that she must go.

She not only continuously heard these voices but she saw shining figures of spirits whom she called saints, as clearly as she saw people. She used to cry when they went away and she wished that they would take her with them. She identified her three chief spirit guides under the names of three saints – Catherine, Margaret and Michael. Later she had said a whole council of angels and the shining cloud came several times every week and at last a voice said "Daughter of God, you will lead the Dauphin (eldest son of the King) to Rheims to be consecrated". Finally came the imperative words, "Daughter of God, go on, I will be with you". At the age of sixteen, she then exchanged her red skirt for a grey doublet and black horse, cut her long hair short and after days of continuous riding she and her little company reached Chinon where the Dauphin was. The Dauphin's advisors were doubtful as to whether he ought to see the Maid but in the end, possibly curiosity prevailed and she was brought to the castle and led up the stairs to a great Hall in which were assembled a company of about three hundred knights and noble ladies in magnificent dress.

Only one man was plainly dressed and directly Joan saw him, she went up to him and kneeling on one knee, she said, "Fair Sir, you are the Dauphin to whom I am come". He, however, hoping to deceive her, pointed to another Knight, who was richly dressed and said, "No that is the King", Then Joan said "No fair Sir, it is to you that I am sent". The Dauphin was much impressed. She was taken to Poitiers to be examined by learned men, priests and lawyers. For six weeks they all tried, in vain, to confuse her by their questions. They then confessed that, "To doubt the Maid, would be to resist the Holy Spirit".

The Dauphin collected an army to march with Joan of Orleans. Clad in white armour, she led the army, riding or running, always in front of them, through a rain of arrows, bullets and cannon balls, waving her banner of Christ and the lilies of France and crying, "Come On".

Many and varied accounts of her clairvoyance were given. One of the most interesting was her prediction that if they would dig behind the altar in the chapel of St Catherine at Fierbois, they would find a buried sword which had been placed there by Charles Marcel. She wished to carry this sword. It was duly found, old and rusty, with five crosses on the blade.

She planned and succeeded in strategies where the best French Army brains had failed. Although wounded herself, she succeeded in four days in delivering the town of Orleans, which for seven months had been besieged by the English. That was on the 8th May. On the 11th June she took the town of Jargeau. On the 15th she took Meun. On the 17th Beaugebcy and on the 18th she destroyed Talbot's chief army at Pathay. On the 17th July the Dauphin was crowned at Rheims.

In short, the four tasks which she had set herself or which had been set for her by her spirit guides, she successfully accomplished. These were to: drive the English in flight: to crown the King at Rheims: to deliver Orleans; and to set free the Duke of Orleans, who was prisoner in England. It was not for twenty more years that the English would be completely driven out of France.

But now comes the tragic and to some people, the inexplicable part of the great story. From the beginning she had known from her spirit guides that her power would only last a year. She was therefore prepared when in the Easter week; suddenly the voices of St Catherine and St Margaret spoke and told her that she would be taken prisoner before midsummer's day: and thus it must be; that she was to be resigned to her fate; and that God would help her. Hence forth she received no further help from her 'voices', who merely reiterated the announcement that she would be captured. Joan knew that this meant being burnt alive, but she continued her divine mission with a faith and with courage greater than ever before. She was now left to her own human resources and was every day, exposing herself to danger but not of death from a sword or bullet, which she would have welcomed. After her trial of witchcraft and many other offences claimed by the English, Joan was put to the most horrible of all deaths – death by torturing flames in Rouen, France on May 30th 1431. – In 1920 Joan of Arc was canonized.

ST. TERESA OF AVILA (A.D. 1515)

Her name in Greek, Tarasia, was in itself a happy coincidence, for it signifies, "marvellous". She was born in the year 1515 of an illustrious old Spanish family. Her mother died when Teresa was a young girl, a beautiful, clever, witty and in every way attractive young girl. She was not unaware of her charms and she seems to have made the most of them, with the result that her father, to safe-guard her from an undesirable love-episode, placed her in a convent.

In prayer she began to be conscious of a Presence and of a Voice which constantly admonished her. She soon found herself living in a supernormal world. She feared that this might be a snare of the devil, at last she unburdened her soul, not to her own Confessor, she did not dare to, but to a Jesuit priest. The priest however showed a rare discretion and told her to take courage, for that possibly through her the Lord intended to do good to many. From that moment, under his guidance, she strode forward on the thorny path of mortification and penance from which she had, up to that time, stood aloof.

One of the most interesting of her experiences was perhaps her vision of the Christ. She describes how at first she 'felt' rather than saw Him, as a cloud-like enveloping the Presence, which for some days, never left her. Gradually it became more defined, until one-day, she being in prayer, the Lord showed her His Hands – His Hands alone, "with such exceeding beauty as is beyond the power of words to describe". A few days afterwards, she continues "I also saw the Divine Face, which left me entirely absorbed in wonder and admiration". "I could not understand why the Lord showed Himself thus by slow degrees". Eventually they led up to a perfect vision of the full figure.

Teresa also had the gift of levitation. One of her Confessors, a learned theologian of the Order of St Dominic, testified to the fact that on one occasion when Teresa was attending a service in the choir of a church, she suddenly felt herself being raised from the ground, and she was obliged to seize hold of a rail to prevent levitation, while she prayed.

As we can imagine, it soon became impossible to conceal from the outside world the marvellous experiences of this Carmelite Nun as they created jealousy and ill-will within the convent. The happenings also created excitement and much criticism outside the Convent walls and she became an object of general observation. The painful element in all this for Teresa was the belief, entertained by the priests and others that these visions and revelations were of the devil. Convinced of their true origin, Teresa suffered martyrdom in having to make a gesture of exorcism with the cross in her hand. One day, she held out the Crucifix of her rosary, the Christ took it from her fingers; and when she received it back, the four large beads of the black ebony were transmuted into precious stones with exceeding brilliancy and on them were engraved the five wounds.

It is clear that Teresa was undoubtedly a great medium, who was not only, like Socrates, a clairaudient by the hearing of spirit voices but that she was gifted with a variety of psychic powers. She was continually liable to trances and often at inconvenient occasions.

 Her writings, what are acknowledged to be works of genius, she believed to be directly inspired and this is the view taken by the Roman Catholic Church, which believes that her books were written under the direct inspiration of the Holy Spirit.

Indeed, all that we are told about the circumstances attending her writings, accords with all that occurs under modern conditions in inspirational writing of today. "When she wrote, says a Prioress, "it was with such rapidity and without stopping to erase or correct, that it indeed appeared miraculous". "Also her face was illumined" says the same Prioress, " by a glorious light, which gave forth a splendour like rays of gold and lasted an hour until twelve at night, at which time Teresa ceased to write and the resplendence faded away from her, leaving her in what, in comparison with it, seemed like darkness".

One night a certain Maria del Nacimiento came into Teresa's cell to deliver a message, she saw some sheets of blank paper on which Teresa had just begun to write, but in the very act of taking off her spectacles to attend to the message, Teresa was carried away in an ecstasy" (trance). When she came to herself, Maria Del Nacimiento noted with amazement that the sheets of paper which beforehand were blank were now covered with handwriting. Where upon Teresa, desirous to prevent her from seeing what had occurred, threw the

"Miraculous manuscript" with simulated carelessness into a chest beside her. This gift was direct spirit writing, writing similar to that which appeared on the wall in the palace at the feast of Belshazzar.

Teresa organized in the remote parts of the country, new Foundations at San Jose, Malagon, Duruelo, Pastrana, Salamanca, and Alba de Tornes, which were, in contrast to those already in existence, dedicated to poverty. She encountered every kind of difficulty – social, financial and physical. But Teresa's psychic faculties assisted her in this work not only socially, morally and financially but also physically. Time after time this now elderly Nun and of the feeblest health was enabled to overcome the difficulties of journeying in rough carts over Castilian mountain tracks and in crossing flooded and bridgeless rivers, by direct supernormal means. For instance, when on her way to Medina, she and her companions were guided to the opposite bank of a flooded river by a light held by unseen hands.

Teresa is an interesting example of the fact that in order to succeed as a leader in the realm of religion, a rare combination of qualities are required, a combination namely of morality, spirituality, will and intellect, plus the psychic faculty. Those who have morality alone remain philanthropists: those who have spirituality alone remain monks or hermits: those with will power alone remain Napoleons in the various spheres of work: those who have intellect alone remain scientists: while those who have psychic power alone, remain mediums.

Though an association of any of these qualities minus

the psychic faculty may produce Leaders who are great in more than one sphere of life, the addition of the psychic faculty to these others is essential in the creation of a great religious leader. Only those who combine with morality, spirituality, will and intellect have the gift of super-consciousness, of a cosmic consciousness, which enables them to penetrate higher planes of thought, and become religious geniuses, reformers, saints, prophets and founders of religion. Teresa died in 1582 at the age of sixty-seven at the height of her fame and it is not surprising to learn that a great and brilliant throng of celestial spirits surrounded her death-bed. Teresa was canonized on the 12th March 1622.

CHAPTER 6

LIGHT IN EVERY TRUTH

GEORGE FOX (A.D. 1624 –1691)

George Fox was indeed a spiritualist if ever there was one. This deadly earnest shoemaker from Leicester, England, in his leather suit was equipped for his revolutionary task. With will power, physical strength, a pair of magnetic eyes and a spiritual truth obtained at first hand. He spent his life stomping round many countries, enduring persecutions, chastisements, imprisonments (in the vilest of dens), that he might convince men of the futility of second-hand religion.

The doctrine that he preached can be epitomized in two words, "Inward Light".

By this he meant the voice of the Divine Spirit in the hearts of men. He differed from the Churches of his day – as spiritualists of this century differ from the Churches of today. Because instead of assuming in the "Divine Spirit", a metaphysical mystery, he gave to these words a literal interpretation. That this Light in very Truth; "lightens every man that is born in this world". And men are hindered from listening for the voice by

Sacerdotalism, which teaches them to rely for grace on things external to themselves and thus their spiritual ear becomes, by disuse – deaf to spiritual sound.

George was born in 1624, in the reign of (James 6th of Scotland) James 1st of England, at a time when the history of England was in a melting pot of change. He remained singularly unconcerned as to the results of worldly battles or Kings. George Fox was the first real democrat in the history of England. At age nineteen, after a series of bad events, which led to prayer, the answer came to him. The Lord spoke and told him he must forsake all, both young and old; he must keep out of all and be as a stranger to all. Then he followed the path like Pythagoras, seeking higher counsel. After four years of study in the various Churches, he still was not quenched in his thirst for knowledge. He then began, as he terms them, his "great openings" or revelations. One Sunday morning, as he was walking and meditating alone in the fields, he heard (clairaudient) a voice which said that, "to be educated at Oxford or at Cambridge was not enough to fit a man to be a minister of Christ. To teach men Hebrew, Greek and Latin, and the seven arts was not the way to make them ministers of Christ".

He began arguing his truths, interrupting the priest that was the cause of his prison term. The length of this imprisonment at Nottingham is un-certain. After his release he again created a similar disturbance in a church in Derby, and was confined in a filthy dungeon for a year. Undaunted , as soon as he was free, he pursued his mission, tramped up and down the country, preaching indoors and outdoors, in season and out of season, breaking in upon courts of justice, public houses, churches, markets, fairs and private houses, throughout England, Scotland and Ireland. Everywhere he proclaimed the great principle that the value of Christianity lies not in its outer forms but in its inner, its esoteric meaning.

Prisons in those days were pest-houses of inconceivable filth and horrors and Fox spent many years within their walls. He was imprisoned at Nottingham (1649), Derby (1650), Carlisle (1653), London (1654) Launceston (1656), Lancaster (1660 and 1663), Scarborough for three years (1666) and Worcester for fourteen months (1674). The charges were blasphemy, heresy, refusing to pay tithes **or** to take an oath and worst offence of all – refusal to doff (take off or tip his) hat. On these various counts 4,500 followers of George Fox at one time during his life, suffered the horrors of imprisonment of which, thirty-two died in prison.

George Fox had considerable psychic powers. He cured disease: he was clairvoyant: he was a discerner of spirits and could exorcise evil spirits: he foretold coming events. While in prison in Scarborough he had "a Divine warning" of the Great Fire of London, which broke out the day after his release. He was given a sight beforehand of the revolution of 1688. A great weight came upon him and the Lord gave him a sight of the great bustles and troubles, revolution and change. Once he was entranced for fourteen days, when he laid, his whole person transformed and he was then incapable of being bled. He had experiences which were beyond the range of the average medium – experiences similar to Pythagoras, Swedenborg and of Jacob Boehme. For example, during a trance the whole of creation was "opened to him and he saw into the natures, into the essence of all things". On another occasion the Lord "opened "to him things relating to those great professions – Law, Physics and Divinity (so-called)." He was shown that the lawyers, doctors and the clergy – by not knowing the inner natures and principles and essences of things – made rules which were not after the wisdom, the equity or the spirit of God.

His disciples also had psychic gifts and signs and wonders accompanied their teaching. They practiced exorcism, prophecy and clairvoyance; they healed the sick; had visions and heard voices and generally exercised the apostolic gifts, though Fox himself regarded such signs and wonders as incidental to his mission.

The psychic power at some of those first enthusiastic Meetings of the Friends must have been tremendous. The whole house in which they sat would shake and on one occasion a clergyman present was so terrified that he ran out of the church afraid that it would fall on him. George Fox busied himself with his pen, writing books and epistles and with the affaires of the ever-growing Society of Friends. In 1677 he paid a short visit to the Continent with William Penn and Robert Barclay to encourage Friends in Holland and Germany and this visit was repeated in 1684. In the interval his time was chiefly spent in London and the suburbs and Home Counties that he may look after Friends suffering under persecutions due to the Conventicle Act. These were only lessened in 1687 by the Declaration of Indulgence.

It was four years later in 1691 that George Fox was finally released from imprisonment of the flesh and obtained that freedom which is mis-named – death, but which is, as we believe, the gateway to eternal life.

EMANUEL SWENDENBORG (1688 – 1771)

Emanuel Swendenborg has been called the greatest spiritualist medium that has ever lived. He was born in Stockholm in 1688, during the reign of Charles X11, who frequently consulted and honoured him. He was the son of a Swedish bishop in West Jutland, who believed in direct inspiration from the spirit world. The name he gave his son must have been an inspiration, for he called him "Emanuel" – God with us "that he might, he said, be constantly reminded of the nearness of God".

Emanuel's early works were on nature. Here follow books on this subject: The Economy of the Animal Kingdom, Anatomically, Physically, Philosophically, and The Animal Kingdom. He received a liberal education and after his University course at Upsala, he followed the fashion of all our great Initiates and travelled to foreign lands. He visited the universities of England, Holland, France and Germany. He journeyed over Europe examining mines and smelting works, always however, deeply studying all the natural sciences upon the supposition 'that with the scalpel of the physicist, he would one day be able to dissect the soul'. His scientific reputation was second to none in Europe. He foreshadowed the nebular hypothesis twenty-one years before Kant and sixty-two years before Laplace. He realized the motor centres in the brain before this was corroborated by the German and English physiologists. He is said to have discovered the atomic theory, the undulatory theory of light; that heat is a mode of motion; that magnetism and electricity are forms of ethereal motion; that molecular forces are due to the action of an ethereal medium.

He was a mathematician, philosopher, physiologist, chemist, engineer, mineralogist, anatomist, astronomer, geologist, psychologist, poet and musician. In all these subjects he made brilliant scientific discoveries. He was practised in various handicrafts such as book-binding, engraving, lens grinding, manufacture of mathematical instruments. He invented also among many other things – a flying machine, a submarine war vessel, a quick firing gun and a mercurial air-pump. He was not the kind of man to be deceived by mental illusions. On the contrary (like St Teresa) he criticized all his experiences with a scientific eye, to guard himself from snares of fantasy and imagination.

At the age of fifty-six years, when presumably he had learned as much of worldly science as was deemed necessary by the higher powers, a change came over him. He had all his life enjoyed extraordinary visions, heard voices and seen lights, but now he received a direct revelation and command – as he believed from the Lord. A spirit appeared to him on two successive nights and on the second night "a certain spirit" spoke and told him that he had been chosen to unfold to men the spiritual sense of the Holy Scripture. "I will myself dictate", said the spirit, "what thou shalt write." That same night the world of spirits – hell and heaven – was convincingly opened to him and from that time forth, he gave up all worldly learning and earthly ambition. He then laboured only in spiritual things according as the Lord command him. Thereafter, he said, the

Lord daily opened the eyes of his soul, to see in perfect observation of what was going on in the other world and to converse, wide awake, with angels and spirits.

Swedenborg had doctrine of what he called, "Universal Correspondency", revealed to him, like Plato's doctrine of "Ideas" was revealed to him. The doctrine, "that things materials are manifestation of things spiritual – the belief that everything outward and visible has an inward and spiritual cause".

He now resigned the post which he had held as Assessor at the Board of Mines and gave himself up to the work for which he had been commissioned, because, he said, "spirits cannot speak with a man who is much devoted to worldly and corporeal cares". But he never regretted the years spent in scientific research on the physical plane. He understood that this study had been necessary in order that spiritual truths might be presented by the light of science, to satisfy reason as well as heart.

His great work, Arcana Coelestia, is an exposition as commanded by the Lord, of the spiritual sense of Genesis and of Exodus. It attributes occult meaning to that which is in the Bible otherwise incomprehensible. It comprised eight volumes, containing 10,837 paragraphs, which were, he claimed, delivered by direct illumination from the Lord.

Swedenborg's life was now spent more with angels, than with men. He was in the world, but not of it. He always, however, sternly refused to use his power of communication with the other world for the purpose of merely gratifying the vulgar or sentimental curiosity of would-be sitters or for any but the most cogent reason. He refused to pander to commercial desire to regain lost articles or to discover hidden treasures. He refused, in short, to prostitute a great gift to unworthy ends. On many occasions his prophesies of visions were proven highly accurate to the minutest of detail. His views of heaven can be corroborated by the modern seers that have journeyed there. He tells us, for instance, that the next world is not a heaven of weary ease but of interesting activities. Education, art, music, literature, architecture, science are earnestly pursued. Man and women live as men and women after death and they take with them to an intermediate state, (where souls are prepared for final abode), their powers and capacities, their beliefs and prejudices.

The spirit-world, indeed, is the same old familiar world as ours "the same old world of God", continued in a higher sphere. Everything with which we are familiar here is perpetuated there. If it be true that material objects are manifestation of spiritual things, then this perpetuation is an understandable fact. Therefore, all that we learn here is not thrown away, but forms the basis of a higher knowledge. "Thus friendships with flowers, birds, rivers, animals, sea and sky, will never be dissolved". Swedenborg, who correctly foretold the day of his death, died in his beloved London in 1771 – aged eighty-four.

ABC of some famous quotations …

John concludes this teaching presentation with a few words taken from well-known quotes as an easy way of introducing philosophy when giving addresses, especially in the first few times of conducting a church service, until addressing the public becomes more familiar. Using them as a starting point often aids or creates the flow of words:

Ancestry – *"I don't know who my grandfather was; I am more concerned to know who his grandson will be"* ~ Abraham Lincoln

Anger – *"An angry man opens his mouth and shuts his eyes"* ~ Cato

"Whenever you are angry, be assured that it is not only a present evil, but that you have increased a habit" ~ Epictetus

Appreciation – *We never know the worth of water till the well is dry* ~ English proverb

Arguing – *"Any fact is better established by two or three good testimonies than by a thousand arguments"* ~ Nathaniel Emmons

If you win all your arguments, you will end up with no friends

Art – *"Every artist dips his brush in his own soul, and paints his own nature into his pictures"* ~ Henry Ward Beecher

Atheism – *"The trouble with atheism is that it has no future. Nobody talks so constantly about God as those who insist that there is no God"* ~ Heywood Broun

Attitude – *"Life is a grindstone; whether it grinds you down or polishes you up, depends on what you're made of"* ~ Jacob M. Braude

Baby – *"A baby is God's opinion that the world should go on"* ~ Carl Sandburg

Begin – *"Great is the art of beginning, but greater is the art of ending"* ~ Henry W. Longfellow

"The beginning is the most important part of work" ~ Plato

Book – *"Books are the quietest and most constant of friends; they are the most accessible and wisest of counsellors and the most patient of teachers"* ~ Charles W. Eliot

Certain – *"Nothing is certain but death and taxes"* ~ Benjamin Franklin

Character – *"In matters of style – swim with the current; in matters of principle – stand like a rock"* ~ Thomas Jefferson

"A man has no more character than he can command in a time of crisis" ~ Ralph W. Sockmann

"Character is what God and the angels know of us; reputation is what men and women think of us" ~ Horace Mann

Charity – *"With malice toward none; with charity for all"* ~ Abraham Lincoln

"The biggest disease today is not leprosy or tuberculosis, but rather the feeling of being unwanted" ~ Mother Teresa

Choice – *"Regardless of circumstances, each man lives in a world of his own making"* ~ Joseph Murray Emms

Conscience – *"Conscience is an inner voice that warns us somebody is looking"*

"The only tyrant I accept in this world is the still, small voice within" ~ Mahatma Gandi

Courage – *"Often the test of courage is not to die, but to live"* ~ Vittorio Lafieri

"Success is not final, failure is not fatal, it is the courage to continue that counts" ~ Sir Winston Churchill

Curiosity – *"Curiosity is one of the permanent and certain characteristics of a vigorous intellect"* ~ Samuel Johnson

"It is better to ask some of the questions than to know all the answers" ~ James Thurber

MEDIUMSHIP: OUR HERITAGE

PART 2

CHAPTER 1

INTRODUCTION OF THE REVEREND JAMES GARFIELD TINGLEY

Reverend James G Tingley D.D. Metaphysician
(Medium extraordinaire) 1923 – 1999

This teaching module was composed by the late Reverend James Garfield Tingley D.D. and is part of the educational programme, for the students attending his classes at the time; an exceptional medium and teacher. I am positive of his delight in knowing that his teaching course is now in print and benefitting students of today in their guidance, in their learning and searching of the origin and methods used in mediumship and its philosophy. In 1992 the Reverend Doctor J. G. Tingley was presented with the first Degree in Honorarium by the Universal Institute for Holistic Studies. Also the Universal Spiritualist Association's Presidents Award (with an addendum) for Fifty-four Years of Distinguished Service to Spiritualism.

The introduction to this valued servant of mediumship is by way of testimonials, written by people who knew

James from boyhood through to the development of his remarkable mediumship:

~~~

The Reverend Fred L. Felix – 1967

"I was glad when they said to me; let us go into the House of the Lord." And so it was, some thirty years ago in 1937, that little Jimmy Tingley, a young lad of fourteen, entered the Episcopal Spiritualist Church of Eaton Rapids, Michigan and sat quietly in the pew as I, a guest minister, conducted services.

The boy's sudden appearance struck me and I couldn't help but wonder what drew this 'Tom Sawyer' type of individual into the services on a Sunday evening when most young boys were at home taking their baths and preparing themselves for the beckoning call of the Monday morning school bell. The lad had entered by himself wearing very modest, but immaculate attire, and in his hand, he carried a sheet of paper.

His curious attention to the service was so intense that I found myself wondering in thought and straying from my presentation. The boy's deep set, magnetic eyes nearly hypnotized me. After all, I was a medium performing in the 'spooky Spiritualist Church where those funny people entered every Sunday night to talk to the ghost and goblins that flew around the building all week.' This was the strange place where that strange preacher held a Halloween party every Sunday night.
~~~

I managed to complete the service in good order, and as I walked up the aisle to the strains of 'God be with us'. The boy's eyes never left my person. He didn't move from his seat until I had bade the parishioners God's blessings. As I shook the last hand, the boy approached me, and in a firm voice he said, "Reverend Felix, would you answer some questions for me?" – "Of course," I replied. And with that, the boy unfolded his sheet of paper on which were written some one hundred well prepared questions regarding the Science and Philosophy of Spiritualism. As I glanced quickly over the many questions, The Rev. John Bunker, Pastor, stood impatiently by waiting to lock the doors for the night. "My God Fred, are you going to answer those questions at this late hour." Immediately, I thought to myself, if this unusual young lad, with his intellectual, curiosity, hidden beneath his Tom Sawyer disguise, had the time and ingenuity to prepare these questions, I certainly had the time to answer them. And so we sat down together.

Thus began a friendship and spiritual bond that has afforded me the unique experience of observing Eaton Rapids own Tom Sawyer grow and develop into a brilliant intellectual metaphysician.

And so it is with personal pride and great pleasure that I introduce to the readers, the man who has been answering 'my' questions for the past twenty years – James Garfield Tingley".

With Sincere Love and Admiration

The Rev. Fred L. Felix

~~~

A New Star in the Spiritualist's Sky
By Gladys E Raymond

"I shall never forget the thrill I experienced the first time I was privileged to witness a demonstration of the remarkable mediumship of the Rev. James G Tingley. The time was late autumn of 1945, the place the Good Fellows Spiritualist Church, 1014 Le Roy St. Jackson, Michigan.

I had heard reports of a young man with ability to bring messages with remarkable clearness, giving names, dates and places, and straightening out complicated relationships with amazing accuracy and rapidity of delivery. But I was in no way prepared for what I saw and heard. Message after message was given which was proof of accuracy to those receiving it, and there was no hesitancy whatsoever on the part of Mr. Tingley – he was absolutely sure of his subject and his delivery was almost machine-gun like in its force and rapidity.

Amazement was written in everyone's face as they listened. He went to one after another, averaging about one message a minute and covering a lot of ground in that minute.

After services that evening, Mr. Raymond and I talked with Mr Tingley and that was the beginning
~~~

of a friendship which continued to this day. In fact, a few months after our acquaintance, when a change took place in his home life, it seemed the natural thing for him to come and live with us and become a member of our household; so I do feel that we do know him rather intimately.

At first, Rev. Tingley served our church one Sunday each month, being at that time a field worker for the I.S.A., of which the Goodfellows Church is an affiliate. On these Sundays, the church was always filled beyond its capacity, the chapel overflowing and extra seats having to be placed in the hall outside the chapel, and sometimes extending into the church parlors.

This arrangement continued for about a year and in January 1947, at the annual election of officers to the Official Board of the church, Mr. Tingley was elected President for a term of one year. The following spring he was retained as regular Pastor, which office he still holds at this time. When his term as President expired, he declined to run for that office again, devoting his whole time to his pastorate, and to his private clients.

After Mr. Tingley took up his residence with us, we witnessed many demonstrations of his outstanding ability of physical phenomena; note; I use the plural term advisedly. Night after night, week in week out, we sat for development and experimental purposes. His trumpet work and direct voice equal his message work. In fact he does not need a trumpet. That instrument merely makes it easier for the spirits to amplify their voices, but even without the trumpet it is nothing unusual for three or four voices to come in simultaneously. If it ever becomes necessary for one of the sitters to move from the circle in the darkness, the trumpet will attach itself to the person in question and forcibly lead them to where they wish to go, and then lead them safely back again to their seats.

On one occasion when Mr. Tingley's daughter Rosalie, who was about three years old at that time, meddled with the trumpet, the spirit forces using the trumpet, picked her up bodily, and placed her on top of a heating stove which is in the room. There was no fire in the stove at the time. This is only one account of many strange happenings which have taken place in our séance room. It would take too much time and space to recount them all.

Rev. Tingley is also a good materialization medium. In fact he is the only one of that phase who can materialize entities without being entranced himself. I witnessed that phenomenon together with five other people, although he usually does go into trance for this phase of his work.

His spirit forms are plainly visible, solid and strong, their voices natural. I remember one séance when Etta Bledsoe materialized, she called little Rosalie up to the cabinet, picked her up in her arms and held her up in the air at arm's length, for quite a minute of time. Perhaps I had better qualify my statement that he is the only medium who can materialize entities without himself going into trance. I should say that as far as I know, he is, never having seen it done by any other, neither have I ever heard of this feat being accomplished by anyone else. However, he has many different phases, card writing and slate writing, apports, healing and a very strange phase (to me) which is photography without camera or film. I saw this done in broad daylight, doors and windows open, sunshine streaming in, and the nearest thing to a circle being the family sitting around the dinner table eating our dinner. All he used was commeo cardboard such as we women use for filing our cooking recipes. We all tried it, with success. Just rub the card between our hands, then hold it to our bodies for a few moments, then behold – the picture, wet with the coloring matter taken from the clothes we were wearing.

I have been a Spiritualist always, have a family background of four generations of believers of Spiritualism, and some of my family have been mediums. I have visited Spiritualist Centers, and observed the work of the finest of mediums, but it is my honest opinion that I have yet to see any medium who has so <u>many</u> phases so <u>well</u> <u>developed</u> as does the Rev. Mr. Tingley. And this opinion is shared by many who know him and are familiar with his fine work."

~ Gladys E Raymond

~~~

James D. Seebach – 1971

"So as stated, this is James Garfield Tingley, who grew up in a little town in Michigan. Jimmy Tingley was the young lad who everyone knew as the corn cob kindling salesman; the billboard advertiser who nailed up the posters for the local theatre. Jim Tingley had an unusual childhood, in that he was the sole support of his family, due to the untimely death of his father. He lived with his Mother Irene and four sisters. Jimmy had two other sisters and a brother, who passed on through the hands of tragedy at early ages. Young Tingley was unusually bright in school and his teachers had difficulty keeping up with him. He graduated far ahead of his classmate's in spite of his reputation as Eaton Rapid's number one truant. Jimmy read every type of printed material he could get his hands on, and at the tender age of twelve, he became interested in psychic things.

At the age of thirteen, young Jim had read that communicating with the so-called dead was based on sensitivity of vibration beyond the range of the physical senses. He reasoned that a dog whistle was audible only to a canine because of its acute sense of hearing. With this is mind, Jimmy commenced to redesign the family's only radio so that it would pick up the more refined frequencies of the Spirit World. After much thought and labor to the project at hand, the boy was ready to talk to his
~~~

first spirit. With the enthusiasm of a Henry Ford, the young genius threw the switch. The machine began to smoke and in a matter of seconds, it blew up before his eyes and Jimmy was immediately convinced that he has contacted 'that other place'!

After his first frightening attempt with spirit communication, Jimmy Tingley sought the help of Fred Felix and other notable mediums of the day. He found fine counsel in the authority of such brilliant psychics as Linguist and Medium, Etta Scott Bledsoe; and The Rev. John Bunker of Eaton Rapids, who gave up the undertaking business to become an outstanding medium because, as in his words, "The mediums in the Spiritualist Church across the street were bringing back the dead faster than I could put them away".

For a short period of time Jimmy Tingley lived in the home of Dr. Julia Walton M.D. Not only was Dr. Walton the first women to receive a medical degree from the University of Michigan, she was a developed medium as was her mother, Nellie McCain. Through Dr. Walton's authority, Jimmy discovered that correct mediumship is advantageous to longevity. A careful examination of the lives of many world renowned psychics will bear this out.

By his fifteenth year, young Jim Tingley was ordained by the Rev. Peter Everett of the National Spiritualist Association and shortly afterwards, Rev. Tingley accepted the Pastorate of the Goodfellows

Spiritualist Church of Jackson, Michigan. He served this church diligently for fifteen years.

Not only did he teach, preach and demonstrate the philosophy and phenomena of Spiritualism, he also prepared dinner every Sunday for fifty to seventy five parishioners, as well as serve coffee and his own made apple pie after each service. On one occasion, I personally helped Jim Tingley prepare a chicken dinner for sixty seven people, which included mashed potatoes and gravy, coleslaw, green beans and his apple pie. The total cost of preparing these dinners was less than a ten dollar bill. How did he do it? His sense of economy is as unique as his genius and gift of phenomena. It had to be in those days when mediums supported themselves on fifty cent readings and one dollar per chair séances.

Between teaching, counselling, dinners and services, Jim Tingley has always found time to further develop his intellect, mediumship and investigative techniques into the unexplained facets of untampered Spiritualism and the psychic sciences. He has developed one of the most unique phases of solid materialization mediumship to be witnessed in recent years; and he has become nationally recognized as one of America's most outstanding test mediums. His ability to lecture extemporaneously on the psychic sciences is unparalleled. His unending endeavour in life is driven by just one ambition, "To prove immortality".

James Tingley has reached a height of excellence in the field of New Age Metaphysics and contemporary, untampered Spiritualism – "The Mother of it all". He has counselled untold numbers from every walk of life including royalty. In 1966 at the invitation of President Clifford Bias, Jim Tingley addressed the Universal Spiritualist Convention at Camp Chesterfield, Indiana. The following year, he was invited to join the staff of that institution where oddly enough, he took up residency in the vacated home of the man who first answered his inquiries regarding the hereafter – Yes! Fred Felix's home.

In 1967, James founded the First Spiritualist Church of Tampa, Florida, which was dedicated by that city's personal representative of the Mayor. In 1969 James accepted the pastorate of the First Spiritualist Church of Toledo, Ohio and within a short period of time, he was invited to lecture in the public school system of Toledo on Metaphysics and E.S.P.

Our psychic friend James Tingley has enlightened thousands of human souls and constantly expresses deep conviction in the biblical statement – "But wilt thou know, O vain man, that faith without works is dead". James Tingley, a man of many moods, is never too busy to listen to any human soul who seeks his counsel. He makes the 185 mile trip from Chesterfield to Toledo every weekend to serve his congregation. Needless to say, the little catacomb at 636 Western Avenue is always filled to capacity, among which may be found university professors, school teachers, business men, journalist and the people who are the closest to Jim Tingley's heart – the working man and his family.

And so this is James Garfield Tingley, Minister, Psychic, Teacher, Metaphysician, Intellectual and above all, Humanitarian.

There is an interesting facet of Jim Tingley's heritage to be noted. In July of 1970, our psychic friend was presented with excerpts from a booklet entitled "LINEAGE OF THE SOCIETY OF THE MAYFLOWER DESCENDANTS OF THE STATE OF RHODE ISLAND", compiled by Ruth Wilder Sherman. This publication indicates that James Garfield Tingley is a direct descendant of the Mayflower Pilgrims who landed at Plymouth Rock in 1620. Jim Tingley did not discover America; however, America certainly has discovered Jim Tingley.

~ James D. Seebach

CHAPTER 2

LET'S GO TO SCHOOL

"What is the nature of a human being? It is a spiritual being in the physical expression to learn by experiences in order to grow the soul"

Rev James G Tingley addressing his students:

Welcome Friends to the first of our tutorials.

Any school of thought must include in its program restrictions for its students to observe. An imposition is placed upon them. The nature of their habits; the previous ways of thinking and all circumstances are affected. They must change; they must adopt the vibrations and environments that best suit their pursuance. It is not an easy task to undertake. Time, patience, determination and all the traits of discipline must be considered. It is advisable to pre-examine their desires or quests very carefully before undertaking its course of achievement. Suitability to the individual and intention of usage of the object are most important to concentrate upon. These problems are far more important than the mystery of the subject understandings and it's mastering. Without proper preparation, attempting such will naturally impair the successfulness of your ambition. Any well-organized class and its course of pursuance are always bounded by a foreign nature of influences. That is, many subjects, detailed problems, adverse psychology and <u>intended</u> determination are injected for the student to labor with. Their value is to bring out thinking and tests or worthiness. A worthwhile quotation is found in Eastern Philosophy: "WHEN STUDENT IS READY, MASTER APPEARS".

<u>SPIRITUALISM</u>   <u>SPIRITISM</u>

Think very carefully on these two words. Which one is the subject of this course? (Know your subject. There must be no confusion.)

WHAT IS SPIRITUALISM?

I want it clearly understood that a definition of conventional nature is not sufficient. I am a positive believer in Spiritualism; <u>UNTAMPERED IN NATURE AND PRACTICE.</u> I am a believer in strict obedience of Natural Law. Every note and beat of the religion, philosophy and science of Spiritualism moves and is Natural Law. Spiritualism is without creed. Creeds are impositions which are binding and promote disorder. It must be understood that I have discarded these theories years ago; for reasons:

(A) Religion cannot be of a supernatural nature in as much as creeds have had their changing effects on man in his pathways of evaluation. Their nature is but the same, only dressed up in modern clothing.

(B) Universal Atonement: This has not come about in the so-called religions. The Law of Attraction must be enforced. For example – Perfect Understanding attracts Perfect Growth. Perfect Harmony creates Atonement and Understanding – all laws dovetailing into one. Perfect Justice Merits Perfect Compensation – thus perfect balance is maintained.

True power properly directed, produces strength and this production is the outcome of Natural Law and its adherence. The manifestation of such power and strength must be projected, from a source of knowledge that has been set into motion. It is and can only be produced by one who has accepted its existence, its presence and its power. <u>It must be found</u>; it must be realized as an entity. Its producing value demands conditions. This entity is, very definitely, indispensable to its progress and function. Your happiness or unhappiness; your success or failure; your welfare and health are affected by this immutable law.

TO THE STUDENT:

The successes of the past labor of the mediumship that I possess are in this lesson and the ones to follow. Further usefulness has prompted me to prepare them for publication. The methods and procedures are new and have been given by the greatest minds in the Spiritual World. I have enjoyed unusual facility in securing the assistance of these Spirit Teachers and I wish to shed a ray of light unto others. I feel that this hour of <u>condemnation</u> of Spiritualistic Phenomena merits all endeavours and corrective help in aiding the sincere student in his or her development.

WHY DARKNESS AND SILENCE?

Much of the phenomena of Spiritualism are practiced in the darkness of a "Séance Room". WHY? Let us first examine the meaning of Genesis and read. "In the beginning, God created the heavens and the earth; the earth was without void and form and darkness was upon the face of the deep."

All the brilliant scientific achievements of Infinite creativeness, which include all nature, life, and the artistics of culture were developed in the silence and the recesses of soil, soul, or concealed housings. The true purpose was to create and develop usefulness. Yet, we must seek its nature; we must fathom the silence and the darkness; wherein we meditate and mature.

None of the phenomena has or will eclipse the psychic eye in the search for truth. The fundamentals of mediumship, the soul's reach and the reach of the mind, are more fascinating than fiction and lore. Let us develop the psychic powers and receive the blessings of God's true Light. This will contribute to the priceless possession of Light.

Meditation is the hour when we can realize the "Sanctuary" of God. All mundane and physical demands are temporarily forgotten. We are, for a moment, *en rapport* with ourselves. The soul expression is allowed to develop and expand. Great light from the inner aura radiates the mind, body and soul. Consciousness is awakened and we retain its intelligent concept after we come back to the physical shrine. The real world of spiritual growth functions within the silence of meditation. Now, enter the silence and plunge into deep meditation. Focus your attention on one objective. The objective is reality of being yourself. The body is but a casing. Andrew Jackson Davis, known as the "Great Seer", called this type of stuff – "That Special Condition". I say, "Special Conditions attract special conditions, such as I just described.

CONDITIONS

Remove yourself from the frustrations of the earth. It can be done. The leisure hours you waste on trivialities can be used for psychic unfoldment. Forget the budgets and ballots; the kitchen and domestic chores. Enter the innermost seat of consciousness. Many times you sense a drifting away of the spirit. Many distant thoughts are clues that you are freeing self from the body. Seated in a cosy room, in a comfortable chair, lights subdued, you will feel far away. You must accredit this many times to vagaries. Yet, I say, you are experiencing

"Soul Projection". Deeper yet still deeper, until the mind, soul and physical consciousness is separated, for a while.

Inspiration is more susceptible when the still quiet hour of the day's occupation is at rest. I have interviewed thousands, whom have experienced great flows of music, writings, poetry and art in the wee small hours of morning. This is the silent hour, when the mind of man is not easily influenced by the dictates of the flesh. Your mental attitude can tear down your mediumship. You must find yourself to bring you in harmony with a chain of power which helps the vibrations, to bring a stronger power and make a stronger force. For example, one piece of cellophane is easy to tear, but a few sheets blended together have greater strength. It is the same with positive and negative thoughts.

You must develop yourselves. Take the skin from your eyes and see your true self. There isn't anything you cannot do if you can overcome your physical conditions. You have donned physical clothing, but you haven't helped your inner-self to develop and become more powerful, so as to hear your guides who will help you. Your guides and teachers want you to go ahead as they progress. We have not as yet demonstrated what we ourselves possess. We are not using all that we have. We must help ourselves and not depend on our neighbour to do the work for us.

MEDIUMSHIP

Psychic phenomena are divided into two classifications. Mental and physical mediumship. Mental phenomena are those subject to the mind's comprehension and susceptibility. The energy used in these phases is derived from the mind.

Examples:

Clairaudience – Clear hearing – the faculty of hearing what is beyond the customary range of hearing

Prognostication – A forecast or predication

Clairgustience – The ability to taste substances outside the range of normal perception

Psychometry – Sensing the history of an object

Clairsentience – Clear feelings of past, present and future states, whether in the flesh or the spirit

Speaking in trance – a condition of semi or total-consciousness allowing spirit the management of mind and energy of the medium for the purpose of communicating with the earth plane

Impressionable mediumship – is being receptive and sensitive to the spirit world's vibration – sensing or being aware of spirits presence.

Xenoglossis or polyglot mediumship – the ability to speak in the language familiar to the controlling spirit when on the earth plane

A physical phenomenon is objective in nature. The power expanded and enforced is basically body structure and comprehended by the five physical senses.

Examples:

Apportation, Precipitation, Direct voice, direct writing, Skotography, Etherealization,

Spirit, photography, Materialization, Transfiguration, Parakinesis and Trumpet

THE DEVELOPMENT OF MEDIUMSHIP

It is very unusual to find obsession and abnormal traits in a person who consciously conforms to the standards of common sense and observes the Universal Law. They must command its attention. It is true that disorder in the vital organs and the impairment of the physical can cause abnormality. However, I sincerely believe that when a situation exists, investigation would show that there had been error committed in the soul composition. There may be room for debate, but let us face facts. We are responsible for conditions we at times deny. Somewhere along the way, error took place. When, where and why is unimportant. The important thing is to try and correct the condition and go on from there. Universal Law states, "God forgives seventy times seven". "The doorway to reformation is never closed to any human soul here or hereafter." Things and conditions don't "Just Happen". There is cause and effect to every thought we demonstrate. Every thought will find fertile soil within the soul expression, it has mind junk and living potential embodied within itself.

Questions have been asked from time to time, is the study and practice of spiritualistic mediumship harmful to the individual? Absolutely not! It is more correct to say, a knowledge and sincere indulgence into mediumship is most helpful and advantageous. The only law to follow is Universal Law and develop only under proper and certain conditions. Know the philosophy, the laws of nature, the principles of mediumship and the proper science of communication just the same as a person of vocation knows their subject. DON'T JUST SIT! Sitting in a dark room will gain nothing for you without the understanding of what you are doing.

Psychic power and the use of it stimulate and refuel the nervous system. It builds up the ego more so than any plasma or exercise known. The brain becomes more susceptible to cellular and psychic response. An active, expressive and psychic function works with the vital organs, allowing them to contact and organize a more perfect union. Actually the universal disorders and conflicts of finite and corporeal nature are due to an uneven balance. Whereas, had psychic action, with psychic direction had been used – vision, success and balance would have controverted errors. I deem it necessary to say, until psychic knowledge is embraced in all schools of learning and practiced, we are going to be under the same old conditions and remain limited.

Black magic, hexing, puerile phenomena, electro-magnetic responses of the mundane and the near astral planes are not the concern of the Spiritualists. Spiritistic taboos and rites of the mumble jumble arts are not associated with the science of communication as taught and practiced by the True Spiritualist.

Devote your attention to the natural flow and the natural response of your need and cultivate not any phases, but only the phase of mediumship that serves your natural growth best. Without this in mind, you will find yourself mixed up and dabbling. You cannot be just anything or anybody you wish to be. The old saying, "Cut out to be "is not in my book. I don't accept this. I believe we must earn what we gain by reaching, evolving and mastering our goals. The Law of Attraction will usher into our lives according to our nature. So be yourself. Don't express a dual nature until you have the power of double action. It is important to rise from the weakness of your words to the strength of your actions. Greatness will come to you without anyone leading you to it.

Defining Universal Law – Everything is connected to everything and everyone is connected to everyone. We are all brothers and sisters with a divine nature, and every thought, belief, word, and action of one affects every being that was, is, or will be (directly and/or indirectly)

CHAPTER 3

A RELIGION OF TRUTH

Spiritualism in the Old Testament

It is the intention and desire to impress upon the student the necessity of understanding the psychic phenomena which is contained in the Christian Bible. It is true that one can find just about anything in the Bible that one is looking for. One gentleman with whom I was discussing the Bible even told that the Bible contained the name of one of the United States. Of course, I did not believe him, but he referred me to the book of Genesis where Noah opened the window of the "Ark and saw" dry land!

In the early 1930's Johannes Greber, a Catholic Priest began to investigate psychic phenomena. He says: "Until I was forty-eight years old, I had never so much as believed in the possibility of communicating with the world of God's Spirits. The day came however, when I involuntarily took my first step toward such communication and experienced things that shook me to the depths of my soul. After I had taken the first step, I could not stop; I must move forward, I must have enlightenment. On I went, treading carefully and bearing in mind the words of the Apostle Paul: 'Test all things, keep that which is good'."

Greber published a translation of the New Testament in 1937, on which he had spent several years in research, unearthing many old documents, but due to the fact that he candidly states that where there was a lapse in original manuscripts which he was able to procure – he asked God to use his mediumship and speak directly to him, filling in those gaps – his translation was not accepted by the Orthodox churches, no more so than was Levi's "Aquarian Gospel" with which many of us are familiar. It is interesting to note that the Orthodox churches do not accept these translations because, presumably, they were partially dictated by the Spirit World, although throughout the Old Testament we read "Thus says Jehovah" or "God Spoke" which is exactly what both Levi and Greber state.

As Spiritualists and as scientists really, for Spiritualism is a philosophy, a religion and a science, we must believe that God's laws and Nature's laws are immutable and unchangeable. In other words what was possible back in Biblical days is possible now, for Jesus said;

> "Verily, verily I say unto you, he that believeth on me, the works that I do, shall he do also, and greater works than these shall he do;"

There may be some questions in your mind as to the validity and accuracy of the Bible, due to so much controversy in recent years, and we do know of course, that the Bible is not infallible. Enough of the history of the Bible will be given to show you why this cannot be, but we do know that it has stood the test of time and we who understand inspirational speaking and writing must realize that much of the Bible was received in that manner and that even as an historical document, it is still of great value to us.

In any study or discussion of the Bible many variables must be taken into consideration, for instance, the language of the day was limited; certain translators have not agreed on all the vocabulary. When Jesus was on earth his native language was Aramaic, although he knew some Hebrew from his studies in the Temple. It is logical to realize that no book could go though as many translators as has the Bible without being colored by the personality of the translators. Another point to be considered is the fact that except in rare cases, the people were uneducated and could not understand, as even our elementary school pupils do today.

Taking all these things into consideration, the fact still remains that at least a third of the human race have accepted it as a sure guide through eternity, believing it to be the inspired record of God's gradual revelation of Himself, His nature, character and will. Yet, it is often forgotten that over 1800 years have elapsed since the last pages of the Bible were written, that it deals with events of the remote past, with races moved by ideas and influenced by a civilization very unlike our own and that the language of much of it has ceased to be a living language for more than 2,000 years. Even the translation which is in common use was made over 300 years ago, at a time when Christian scholars had only just become conversant with Hebrew and it is also only within fairly recent years that travellers have familiarized themselves and others with Eastern scenes and customs.

We hear all sorts of criticism and all sorts of crazy interpretations of passages in the Bible – for instance, a lady came to me for a reading. Apparently she was an intelligent, cultured person, she certainly looked so. After several minutes, when I asked if she had any other questions, she took my breath by stating very emphatically that she knew, without a question of doubt, that after death we lived on in the spirit world but we assumed the form of animals. Of course, I told her she was surely mistaken and asked where she got that idea. She told me from the Bible, because it distinctly stated that the sheep would be separated from the goats!

It is hoped from this tuition, for you the student, to gain a practical psychic understanding of many of the passages in the Bible that have not heretofore been clear, and our reason for this is simple – most of us, whether we accept the Bible as the word of God or not – came into Spiritualism through the orthodox churches and most of the criticism of Spiritualism comes from members of the orthodox churches. In other words, a study of these old psychic stories of the Bible furnishes us with the approach to people who have been reared on the Bible and therefore, it befits us as Spiritualists, to be able to explain these passages.

The Bible is a psychic book; its pages are full of references to spirits and angels. It constantly carries a message of spirit communication between our world and the future condition of existence. The so called supernatural events which are found within its pages are to stir us to wonder and speculation regarding our future state, about the nature of God; about our destiny and our eventual happiness. Since many people take the Bible as an authority, we must seek the true interpretation of its statements. Our reasoning, faculties, together with our present day experiences, scientific or otherwise, must determine for us the truth and the logic of what the Bible tells. This book of Jewish and Christian law is a Decalogue of universal spiritual laws. We cannot find its entire interpretation solely through a single creed or combination of creeds. We must seek a universal understanding of spiritual truths. If it were not for our present knowledge and experience of psychic phenomena, we would be unable to understand most of the stories that have come down to us from ancient times, but present psychic knowledge makes it easy to understand their meaning.

The Bible, as we all know, consists of two parts; The Old Testament, written in Hebrew, containing the Law, the Prophets and the sacred writings. The Pentateuch is the Hebrew version of the first five books of the Old Testament, said to have been written by Moses.

The Old Testament is more or less a history of the Jewish people but the Bible records differ greatly from the secular history in that all other interests are entirely subordinated to the religious one. Hence public events are devoted to the records of spiritual experience.

The earliest known books of the New Testament were

written in Greek, but we know that most of the original manuscripts were in Aramaic. It now consists of the four Gospels, the Book of Acts, the Epistles of Paul, other writings of the Apostles and the Book of Revelation.

To get a clearer understanding of the Bible, I think we should review its history just a little. Most of us use the King James Version of the Bible, authorized by King James, early in the 16th century. Before King James Version was published there had been 1000 years of controversy and 1000 years of attempted translation, during which time all the original manuscripts had been scattered or lost. (See later the Chapter on the Dead Sea Scrolls).

In 150 BC, 72 men came together and in 72 days acquired the book, known as the Old Testament and translated it from Hebrew* and Aramaic to Greek.

About 376 AD, at around the time when the Catholic Church was gaining ground, just before the Fall of Rome, another translation, known as the Vulgate Bible, was made by Jerome, then Bishop of Spain. Damasus was Pope and he ordered Jerome to do the translation. During the recent trouble in Spain some correspondence was unearthed in an old monastery purported to be between Damasus and Jerome, in which Jerome frankly admits that he inserted certain passages which were not found in any previous translation, in order that they might lend authority to practices of the Catholic Church at that time. Damasus ordered the Council of Trent to decree that Jerome's Bible was

***

*   Hebrew is very similar to Aramaic

inspired. When these documents were found, the Pope of Rome declared that such passages as Jerome inserted must remain because he considered them as having been inspired by the Holy Ghost.

In 1385 came the Wycliff translation and in 1526 William Tyndale laboriously printed copies on a crude printing press and finally in 1600 the King James Version was authorized – all going back to the Vulgate. There were forty-eight translators, and only two of them were Jewish or Hebrews, and they passed to spirit before the work was finished. In 1611 the King James Version was published and this version we use today. However, the latest Revised Edition which was given to us a few years ago changes certain passages. It is interesting to learn that the words shown in Italics in the St. James Version were those words about which meaning was doubtful. My purpose in going into this history as completely as I have is not to cause you to doubt the Bible – not at all, for whether we believe it or not, we are influenced by it. It is interesting too, to learn that whenever an agnostic has made a comprehensive study of this work, he has come away believing in it.

Before we start on our study of the psychic phenomena of the Bible, it seems to me that it is really necessary for us to understand the terms used in scripture. There are so many different terms used to designate the same thing that they become confusing, so here you will find a list of expressions or biblical terms and their present day meanings.

1.   Spirits

The Spirit

Lord

Lord God

God

Ghost

Angels of the Lord

Angels of Heaven

Angels

Men in Bright Clothing

1. (Meaning – A Spirit entity, usually a communicating Spirit)

2.   Word of God

Word of the Lord

2. (Meaning – The Spirit Message)

3.   Man of God

A Prophet

A Seer

One who hath Familiar Spirits

3. (Meaning – A Medium)

4.   Holy Ghost

The Comforter

The Spirit

The Lord

I am

Yahweh

Jehovah

4. (Meaning – A Spirit Control – a spirit teacher or guide)

Many of us were brought up with the idea that the Bible was the word of God, infallible and irrevocable, and many people believe that the Bible condemns Spiritualism, whereas in reality it teaches Spiritualism. Many of us as children had family prayers in the morning, when father would read a chapter out of the "Good Book" then utter a long prayer which had no meaning for us as children and who could only think of the cereal which would be cold before we could eat it. Personally, I had to read one chapter of the Bible every day and five chapters on a Sunday. In this way one could read the Bible all the way through in one year, which my mother did every year. I'm afraid I didn't get too much understanding out of the Bible as I had to read it as a child.

There were too many conflicting statements – too much of fear and that just didn't seem logical to me. I remember the story of a man who had gotten into serious financial difficulties and when he consulted his Pastor, he was told to open the Bible at random and put his finger on a verse without looking; The man did this and read with a great deal of horror – "And Judas went and hanged himself" – Thinking that God would surely help him out of that one, he tried again and read, "Go Thou and Do Likewise". This is only a story of course, but many people of a generation ago felt that this was a means of learning God's will.

Percy J. Hitchcock, in his *Psychic Bedside Book*, tells of asking his father to explain some particularly horrible Bible story which had engulfed his childish imagination and his father answering, "My boy, when you have a haddock for breakfast what do you do? You take out the bones don't you? Well, do the same with those parts of the Bible which you cannot swallow".

That is all very well and good advice – but how much better it would have been to have had a psychic understanding, for after studying and analysing psychic law and then reading the Christian Bible we must come to the logical conclusion that it was written by Spiritualists for Spiritualists even though the term Spiritualism was unheard of at that time. It is truly a psychic book and must be psychically interpreted to be understood.

We are greatly criticized by some orthodox theologians because we believe that a spirit produces raps on a table or wall as methods of communication or for the use of a crystal for concentration – but those who study the Bible with the knowledge of psychic phenomena can prove many such instances

Several passages of the Old Testament relate to Miracles, Clairvoyance and Clairaudience. Our first reference is found in Exodus, Chapter 3, Verse 2 – and it is the story of Moses and the Burning Bush. This may be presented both as a miracle and also as clairvoyance and clairaudience. Right now I wish to interject that Spiritualism does not accept the word "miracle" in its literal sense, which means "supernatural". The Spirit Teachers have told us that all happenings in this world and the Spirit World are governed by Natural Law and there can be no happenings above or beyond this law for it is God's Law. Therefore the word super-natural is, to our minds a misnomer.

No doubt some of the so-called miracles of the Bible were meant to be symbolical while others were brought about by the action of a law not then understood by the people. The early priests believe that the more mysterious and incomprehensible were the rites of the church the more interested were the people and this strengthened their hold over them. This is still true in the present day and age, for there are many people today who would rather believe in a religion which they do not understand than to believe in one that is logical and in harmony with Nature's laws. Many seem to be afraid to believe in a religion that can be analysed, classified and proven by science. The wide breach between theology and science has been caused by the fact that the church has tried to force science to accept things which cannot possibly be proven by the action of the law upon which science bases its findings. The Old Testament, especially, is filled with these so-called miracles and of course I will not have time to cover them all but if we can arrive at an understanding of even a few, it will be of help.

(Spirit Lights)

Let us look at Moses and the Burning Bush – we read "And the angel of the Lord appeared unto him in a flame of fire out of the midst of a bush and he looked and behold the bush was not consumed". In the light of psychic understanding, this will not prove too difficult for us to understand. We often see spirit lights that are like tiny flames in almost every séance and sometimes a flash of light seems to permeate the entire room. Occasionally we see a glow of light about the medium or teacher who is working for the spirit people and the Greek literature tells us that Pythagoras was enveloped in a glow of red light whenever he talked to the people in the temple. Now the spirit who appeared to Moses out of the bush was no doubt trying to attract his attention in order that he might give Moses instructions as he, Moses, had been chosen to lead the Jewish people out of the bondage in Egypt.

(Vibrations)

We learn that Joshua was standing outside of the walls of Jericho when a spirit gave him directions as to how he should take the City. That he and the people should shout and priests blow their trumpets and the walls fell flat. Obviously, the people present did not understand the laws of vibration but the spirit did. He knew that the combined vibrations of trumpets and the voices of the people would shatter the walls of Jericho. We know of many instances where vibration can cause damage – for instance, glass is often shattered from an explosion many miles away and officers commanding a company of soldiers always order them to break step when they are crossing a bridge, lest they damage it by the combined vibrations of their footsteps and cause it to fall. The story is told of one of our great singers, who when giving a recital in Carnegie Hall. A man in the audience noticed that with her high notes the huge chandelier had been loosened and was about to fall.

The recital had to be stopped to permit reinforcement.

We, who understand even a little about psychic law, know that the spirit people are able to change the vibration of matter as is proved to us by the production of apports and by the dematerialization of matter. It is quite possible that the spirit who instructed Joshua about the fall of the walls of Jericho would be able through an ectoplasmic force, to change the vibrations of the foundations of the wall so that the collective sound of shouting voices and the blast of the trumpets could cause it to collapse. That these events can happen has been proved by psychic investigators under the strictest test conditions.

Now let us see what there is in the Old Testament concerning materialization. In Exodus we read:

> "And the Lord went before them by day in a pillar of a cloud to lead them the way; and by night in a pillar of fire, to give them light; to go by day and night".

Those of us who have sat in a séance room and have seen ectoplasmic forms can certainly understand this, for often the forms in a séance room in their flowing ethereal robes do look like a pillar of cloud. We have also seen spirit forms in the séance rooms that wear spirit lights so bright that they might be likened to a pillar of fire. So these things are logical and understandable to a spiritualist.

While, of course it would be impossible to cover all

the phases of mediumship demonstrated in the Old Testament, I am sure that what has been covered so far will give enough proof of the fact that all phases of mediumship, known and demonstrated today, were a part of the religious teachings of the people of old. Knowing that these things were prevalent in Ancient days, no one can consistently deny their reality today. They were made manifest through a demonstration of Natural Law and the same law can be manifested today if we have the 'instrument' – the medium – the prophet – through whose instrumentality the phenomena is possible.

Let me mention the mediumship of Daniel. We are told that he was entranced:

> "And I Daniel, alone saw the vision; for the men that were with me saw not the vision, but a great quaking fell upon them, so that they fled to hide themselves".

Perhaps you may recall that in the early history of the Quakers there was quaking and shaking of the people when they were inspired by the spirit, so this too we can understand. Really, there is little difference between the trance mediumship of Daniel's time and that of our present day. We have many mediums whom the spirit guides are able to entrance and speak through, just as did the spirit when he spoke through Daniel. Many valuable and evidential communications have been received through this phase of mediumship.

We Spiritualists must recognize the fact that although

the Old Testament is filled with many instances of psychic phenomena, it really portrays <u>Spiritism</u> and not <u>Spiritualism.</u> There is a great difference in the meaning of these two terms. A Spiritist is one who believes in spirit communion but a Spiritualist is one who believes in the Science, Philosophy and Religion of Spiritualism. War, hatred, fear, slaughtering etc., which was taught by the prophets of the Old Testament, finds no counterpart in the beautiful teachings of the Man of Galilee upon which Spiritualism bases its philosophy. A true Spiritualist is one who strives to live, according to the highest teachings of our philosophy and religion, based upon spirit communication, by means of Mediumship.

The Old Testament has many references to various phases of mediumship and at the same time, so many contradictions that there is little wonder that people who have no psychic understanding, and have never studied Spiritualism and the laws that govern spirit communion, become hopelessly confused. Nearly every book in the Bible and a large percentage of their chapters discuss matters which can be understood only by studying them in the light of Spiritualism. For instance, the Bible mentions angels ministering to man in 248 different places. We know that not only does Spiritualism prove and explain the unusual stories of the Bible but in turn will be found to give authority and substantiation to Spiritualism.

In Exodus the spirit gave Moses detailed instruction on how to make his spirit cabinet. It was covered with gold within and without and was the most sacred possession of the Israelites. His cabinet had curtains the same as modern day séance cabinets, only his were inlaid with gold. Of course no modern medium could afford the expense of gold linings or gold furniture for their cabinets but Moses was better paid than most mediums. Mediums are often criticized for accepting money for their services; however the spirit instructed Moses to collect half a shekel from every one of the Israelites who were over 20 years old "as an offering unto the Lord". One half of a shekel is about 30 cents in our money and since there were over 600 thousand men over 20 years old, this collection was approximately $181,000. Apparently Moses was well paid for acting as a medium. It is really amusing when we consider that right here in this land of religious liberty, orthodox Christians, who claim to believe in the Bible, pass laws condemning spirit communication and call it "fortune telling".

In the 33rd Chapter of Exodus we have evidence of a dark trumpet séance, it reads:

> "And it came to pass, as Moses entered into the tabernacle, the cloudy pillar descended and stood at the door of the tabernacle and the Lord talked with Moses"

This cloud of ectoplasm shut out the sight from the congregation. Some spirits manifest better in the dark than the light, and evidently this was the case with the Spirit Jehovah, for the interior of the cabinet was dark.

In the 27th Chapter of Numbers it reads, five women have readings with Moses. These women wanted to consult the Spirit Jehovah regarding business – is this fortune-telling? No it is professional mediumship and can be constituted as "private consultations" such as mediums offer today. The Old Testament is filled with references to prophecy, in fact one cannot read its pages without being convinced that the people of those days firmly believed in prophets and prophecy, and that they relied upon their prophets and were at a loss when they did not have an opportunity to consult them.

> "And it shall come to pass afterward, that I will pour out my spirit upon all flesh; and your sons and your daughters shall prophesy; your old men shall dream dreams, your young men shall see visions". (Joel 2:28)

This is only one of the many instances where the spirit has promised that the people shall be filled with the Holy Spirit (the spirit power) and shall be able to prophesy and discern spirits.

We conclude The Old Testament with reference to trumpet speaking of which there are many but I will cover just one. Moses received the Ten Commandments (through slate or independent writing). However, if we read Chapter 19 of Exodus, we discover that these same commandments were first given by spirit voice through a trumpet. This chapter tells of Moses meeting "the Lord" (apart) upon the mount and the spirit comes in a thick cloud. Undoubtedly that cloud was formed of the substance we know as ectoplasm.

> "And it came to pass on the third day in the morning,

that there were thunders and lightening's, and a thick cloud upon the mount, and the voice of the trumpet exceeding loud; so that all the people that was in the camp trembled". "And when the voice of the trumpet sounded long and waxed louder and louder, Moses spake and God (the spirit) answered him by a voice."

This was indeed a dark séance.

When we read and discuss these happenings, we cannot help but wonder at the inconsistencies of man. How many people do you know who believe absolutely in the words of the Bible and yet say it is not possible for a spirit voice to come through a trumpet? They laugh and poke fun because a trumpet séance is held in the dark and yet here is direct evidence of the fact that darkness was necessary for a trumpet séance, even through the medium Moses.

~~~
~~~

CHAPTER 4

THE MASTER MEDIUM

HE WHO INSPIRES

Although spiritualism accepts the Christian Bible, it places more importance upon the New Testament, as its philosophy is based upon the Sermon on the Mount and the teachings of the Man of Galilee.

Again, I must urge students to remember that the books of the Bible were written by many different men and are saturated with personal beliefs. To be of value to the people who lived at the time they were written, they had to contain a solution of their particular problems and because of the different translations much of the original meaning has been entirely changed. The prophets of the age in which the Old Testament was written were obliged to give lessons of moral value in symbolic form that their people could understand, but those who later translated the Bible have interpreted many of these symbols literally and have thus created much confusion. This has caused many scholars to say that a statement can be proven in one part of the Bible and denied in another part.

Theology teaches us that Jesus was of miraculous birth, the only Son of God. Many Spiritualists disagree among themselves as to whether or not Jesus was of miraculous birth. Some Spiritualists say that since Spiritualism is based upon Natural Law, he was of natural birth, the same as all other men. Other Spiritualists think the miraculous birth was possible – personally, I don't think it matters a bit one way or the other. We believe the Spirit is capable of doing many things which seem difficult for us to understand and while it hardly seems possible, it could be – so I prefer that each of you would draw your own individual conclusions about this very controversial matter.

Spiritualism, however, does not believe Jesus to be the only Son of God, for it teaches that all are the children of God and Jesus is our Elder Brother. Many feel that Jesus did not consider himself to be of miraculous birth for we find evidence in the Bible that he repeatedly called himself the Son of Man. In Luke 9, we read:

> "Saying, The Son of Man must suffer many things and be rejected of the elders and the chief priests and scribes and be slain, and be raised the third day".

In Matthew, Mark and John we find similar evidence that Jesus did not believe himself to be the Son of God.

We do believe however, that Jesus was endowed by God with a dynamic message to mankind. It was his mission to prove to all men the continuity of life, the communion of spirit and to teach men to love God, rather than to fear Him.

Spiritualists believe that we are all of one spirit (God) and that the same spirit dwells within each of us, the difference being in the degree that we manifest our God qualities.

Jesus recognized fully his relationship to the Father and he was a Master in the art of right living. It is quite evident that he taught his disciples not to fear death for they fearlessly faced death many times. That he must sacrifice his life and prove his teachings by returning himself was a foregone conclusion. That his psychic ability was understood by his disciples and that many of them developed phases of mediumship is quite evident in the New Testament.

The truths which are taught by the various Christian denominations are based chiefly upon the writings of the New Testament. Flawless and unassailable evidence must therefore be produced to prove that the contents of these texts were indeed revealed by God.

Into what category do the writings of the New Testament fall? All other Christian churches teach that the narratives and the epistles of the New Testament were imparted to their respective authors by the "Holy Ghost" through inspiration, that is to say, by way of "Dictation". What proofs have churches for this doctrine? There are two ways in which it could be proved, one being an express statement on the part of the authors of the New Testament to the effect that the contents of their records and epistles were dictated to them by the Spirit of God.

Do the authors themselves say that their writings were imparted to them by the "Holy Ghost"? They, if anyone, must have known whether they were writing the story of their personal experiences and observations, or whether they were only being employed as "instruments" by God's Spirit. If they wrote their accounts on their own impulse in a purely human style, they would, quite naturally, make no special mention of the fact. If, however, they acted merely as "instruments of God's Spirit", they were duty bound to acknowledge the fact and give the credit to God.

Of the books in the New Testament only one was communicated by an angel – The Revelation of John. John stresses this fact in the opening of his book. The authors of all the other books of the New Testament say nothing about the operation of any supernatural influences upon the writing of their reports. Luke, on the contrary, expressly states in the first few lines of his gospel that he has compiled his story in quite the ordinary human way. He writes –

> "Many before me have undertaken to write the story of the well-established events that happened among us".

John declares that he himself witnessed the events that he relates and it is understood that Matthew and Luke witnessed much of their story and Mark, whom Bible authorities tell us was a small boy at the time, may have remembered a great deal of what he writes.

We must bear in mind that the various epistles were written by the Disciples and Paul and they deal with contemporary matters and were occasioned by inquiries and reports that were pertinent to the Christian congregations <u>at that time.</u>

All this implies no denial of the fact that a spirit from God carried to the apostles those Christian truths that appear here and there in their epistles, however – we must remember that these epistles were written late in the lives of the men and could not be absolutely as they happened, but rather as they <u>remembered</u> them. Naturally, there had to be many things which were not exactly as they happened. In other words, we must take into consideration the human element. The authors of the narratives in the New Testament wrote of their own choice and on the basis of their purely human knowledge, with the exception of the Revelation of John. Some wrote eye and ear–witnesses, others had made careful investigation among people who had witnessed the events and therefore their writings laid claim to trustworthiness as long as the reports which were lost, made by them were extinct. But remember the original manuscripts were lost many centuries ago and that Jesus did not leave anything in writing.

Remember too that the Orthodox Christian Churches contend that the New Testament was an inspired work and the only source of divine truth. If that were so then the New Testament would contain all the truths that Jesus wished to reveal to mankind. The fact is, however, that while he was on earth he had many important truths that he could not reveal to his disciples because they were unable to understand them. He very clearly stated that he would send them, spirits of truth, who would teach them.

It is an actual fact that no other book on earth has undergone so many changes and alterations at the hands of the copyists, the old scribes, as has the Bible, both the Old and New Testaments. Even the well versed Bible scholar cannot say for certain which, are the words, sentences or chapters that have been intentionally or accidentally left out, overlooked, misread, and misinterpreted by the copyist. Furthermore, not one of the scribes who made the copies that we have today, including the new translation, had access to the original text but only to copies of the still earlier copies!

Most important is that for 1600 years the world of God's spirits has been sort of lost in the shuffle. The leaders of the churches have discounted spirit communion, which we know was a definite part of the early Christian Church. But wherever God's spirits have been forced to give ground, others appear. Remember Paul writing to Timothy – "God's spirits expressly declare that in times to come many will fall from faith and turn to spirits and doctrines of deceit".

I only wish that I had the time to go into all the history of the New Testament in order to show how much of it was influenced by the Essenes, the Gnostics etc., and their doctrine of a Universal Spirit, the Avatar of which was Jesus – and how the first teachings of Jesus were gradually changed – but time does not permit.

We can all fervently pray that the time will not be far distant when the religion of the early Christians will be given back to the people, when the spiritual burdens that have been imposed on their shoulders by man-made teachings will be lifted and no longer craving for power – thus resorting to us our freedom to commune with God's spirits, the bearers of the truth. Then we will see how great an influence Christianity can and will exert on the people of today, as it did upon the people of the early days. In the long run it is only the truth that creates power.

> Matthew – "When they had heard from the King they departed; and lo, the star which they saw in the East, went before them till it came and stood over where the young child was. When they saw the star they rejoiced with exceeding great joy".

We know from our teachings that God's laws are unchanging and immutable and that Nature's laws are likewise and therefore we know that a star could not change in its course even to lead wise men to the birthplace of the Holy child. This star was, undoubtedly a spirit light produced by the Higher Forces of the Spirit World to lead these men to the Babe. In our séance rooms and even in our homes, we are often privileged to see these psychic lights that donate the presence of some spirit guest. We must remember that Jesus left no written word and the four Gospels of Matthew, Mark, Luke and John, are the only records we have of his birth and teachings and these were written some 30 to 40 years (and some historians even say 100 or 200 years) after the crucifixion. The reason that nothing was written is because the people expected Jesus to return to earth to be their <u>temporal</u> King. When years passed without his returning in person, they began to realize that he referred to a <u>Spiritual</u> Kingdom and to realize that some record of his life and teachings must be given to posterity.

It seems to me that it would only be natural for the Disciples to surround the birth of Jesus with mystery for he rose from the dead and walked among them after his crucifixion, appearing at least ten times before his ascension and surely, according to his disciples, with their limited understanding at that time, no man born of woman could do this. It is quite logical too that one sent with such a message to mankind would be protected by the Higher Forces until his mission was accomplished. When we consider that his three short years of teaching and demonstrating truths have given mankind a religion that has endured for nearly two thousand years, we surly can understand the importance of his ministry.

Matthew tells us of the vision of Joseph "And being warned of God in a dream that they should not return to Herod they departed into their own country another way".

King Herod had heard of the birth of Jesus and all Jerusalem knew of the ancient prophecy regarding the coming of the Messiah that should rule Israel. Herod was most disturbed. He was determined that the child should not live, so sent the Wise Men to Bethlehem instructing them to search for the child and bring him word of his whereabouts that he too might worship him. The Spirit Forces which surrounded the baby Jesus certainly knew of Herod's intentions to have him put to death. The Wise Men had found Jesus and had departed another way when Joseph was warned in a vision:

> "And when they were departed, behold, the angel of the Lord appeared to Joseph in a dream saying arise and take the young child and his mother, and flee into Egypt; and be thou there until I bring thee word; for Herod will seek the young child to destroy him".

We all remember the story of how when King Herod realized that the Wise Men were not coming back to tell him of the birth of Jesus he become desperate and ordered the death of all male children in Bethlehem under the age of two years. Joseph outwitted him, however, for he had already obeyed the voice of Spirit and had taken the child and his mother and fled. He remained in Egypt until Herod died and then Joseph received a further vision:

> "But when Herod was dead, behold an angel of the Lord appeared in a dream to Joseph in Egypt, saying arise, and take the young child and his mother and go into the land of Israel; for they are dead which sought for the young child's life".

Joseph obeyed the Spirit and started out for Israel but hearing that the son of Herod was reigning in his place, he became alarmed.

"Being warned of God in a dream, he turned aside into parts of Galilee. And he came and dwelt in the city called Nazareth; that it might be fulfilled which was spoken by the prophets – He shall be called a Nazarene".

Now to Spiritualists, there is nothing mysterious about the visions of Joseph, nor the birth of Jesus, for it is in harmony with Natural Law as we understand it, and that law is still being demonstrated today as it was nearly 2000 years ago. I have gone into some detail concerning the birth of Jesus and the psychic phenomena surrounding it, because it is felt that there has been such a lot of controversy over it.

Many of you will wonder at some of the explanations I give of the various phenomena told in the Bible. Some of you will accept and some of you will not – that is to be expected. If this course of lessons on the Bible makes you think a little, perhaps alter some of your old moth-eaten conceptions, and I say this advisedly – for the study in which I indulged to bring them to you certainly changed many of mine – and if it does this, then I will be happy, for we are bound to change our opinions. The philosopher humorously said:

"We used to think the world was flat, with a very large place to fall off at. But now we know it is not that, it is just a place to live life at".

So let us try and change our conceptions – in the first Chapter of Luke we read about John the Baptist who was born just six months before Jesus. The story of his birth is so closely interwoven with that of Jesus that it is well for us to be familiar with the psychic happenings surrounding both.

Zacharius, the father of John the Baptist, was a priest in the temple and he and his wife Elizabeth had long wanted a son but none had been born to them. One day as Zacharius was burning incense in the temple he saw standing at the altar, a spirit, an "angel of the Lord" and the spirit told him that his prayers would be answered and he would have a son whom he should call John. Luke tells us that this angel was Gabriel, the same spirit that later appeared to Joseph and Mary and foretold the birth of Jesus. According to the prophecy of the angel, Elizabeth did conceive and when she was into her sixth month the angel appeared to her cousin Mary and prophesied the birth of Jesus.

That John was destined to be guided by Spirit is quite evident as Luke wrote:

"And he shall go before him the spirit and power of Elias to turn the hearts of the fathers to the children, and the disobedient to the wisdom of the just; to make ready a people prepared for the Lord".

Of course we know that Elias had been in the spirit world for many years and it is logical for us to believe from this statement that they expected John to be guided by the spirit Elias. We are told that "John grew and waxed strong in spirit and was in the desert until the day of his shewing (showing) into Israel". Surely while John was in the desert, he was developing his mediumship, being prepared for the work he had chosen to do, by the Spirit Forces. We are also told that John was preaching and baptizing in the country round about Jordan. The people knowing the old prophecy were attracted to him and many of them wondered if he was the Messiah. His answer:

> "I indeed baptize you with water, but one mightier than I cometh, the latchet to whose shoes I am not worthy to unloose. He shall baptize you with the Holy Ghost and with fire".

It seems logical to think that since John and Jesus were second cousins, that John would have known since childhood that Jesus was the Christ that had been prophesied and when Jesus came to him for baptism he hesitated because he felt himself to be unworthy.

We learn very little about the childhood of Jesus, although most of us know the story of how he counselled with the doctors and the Priests in the Temple and how amazed they were at his knowledge. Jesus must have been aware at an early age of the prophecy of his future and mission and he knew that he must be preparing for that work.

The four gospels tell us little of Jesus after this contact with the priests and wise men at the temple but psychic revelations lead us to believe that during the interval between this time and his baptism by John, that he was being prepared by the Higher Forces for his coming message to the people of Israel. At the age of 30 Jesus came to John to be baptized. As I wrote a moment ago, John knew Jesus was destined to become far greater than he and when Jesus asked to be baptized he said:

"I have need, to be baptized of thee and comest thou to me?"

So John baptised him and has he rose out of the water we are told that the heavens were opened unto him and he saw the Spirit of God descending as in the form of a dove and lighting upon him. The story of the baptism ends with:

"And lo, a voice from heaven saying, this is my beloved son, in whom I am well pleased".

I am sure that we can all agree that this was a psychic manifestation made possible through the mediumship of these two wonderful psychics. Evidence has lead us to believe that the audible spirit voices, spoken of so many times in the Bible, were undoubtedly the voices of the prophets or guardian angels, as it were – for surely if we have guardian angels they would most likely be our loved ones already passed to spirit or the spirit teachers who had been assigned to teach and guide us. In the light of this understanding, the voice which spoke from Heaven, saying: "This is my beloved son, in whom I am well pleased," could have been the voice of Joseph, his father, for surely he would have been well pleased, or it could have been the voice of Elias, whom many thought to be Jesus's spirit guide.

When Jesus sought the mountain top and bade his

disciples to follow him, that which he taught them has become to us as "The Sermon on the Mount" and contains the basis for the philosophy of the religion of Spiritualism. His teachings here in this famous sermon contain the explanation of God's natural law as we understand it today. Jesus knew the laws governing right living and he demonstrated them perfectly in his ministry. This seems to be conclusive evidence that Jesus believed that God's laws are unchangeable and that which was demonstrated by him could be done by others if they followed the law. We know that Jesus was able to produce materialization for The New Testament gives us many instances.

Jesus knew that the time for his crucifixion was drawing near and undoubtedly felt the need of guidance from his Spirit teachers. He called Peter, James and John and they went up onto the high mountain. Jesus evidently knew that these three were ready for the phenomena they were about to witness.

Mark tells us that Jesus was transfigured:

> "And his raiment became shinning, exceeding white as snow; so as no fuller on earth can white them". "And there appeared unto them Elias with Moses; and they were talking with Jesus". "There was a cloud that overshadowed them; and a voice came out of the cloud, saying: "This is my beloved Son, hear him".

The spirit voice speaking out of the cloud of ectoplasm and the materialized forms of Moses and Elias were too much for the disciples to bear and they fell on their faces in fright. Jesus came to them and touched them and told them not to be afraid and when they looked up again Jesus was alone.

I mention this particularly because here we see the result of fear vibrations on an ectoplasmic formation. We know that fear and doubt are most destructive to any physical phenomena and the first materialization that one sees is truly an awe-inspiring spectacle and one can easily understand the fear of the three disciples. It is regrettable that the early Christian church gradually grew away from the acceptance of the manifestation of physic power and taught its followers that the so-called miracles of the Bible were produced by the early prophets but ceased at their death. Fortunately there have been many mediums able to produce materialization. This consists of the production of an ectoplasmic replica of the former human body of the spirit entity by means of physical mediumship and conclusive evidence that the so-called dead can return and give proof of the survival of the human personality. This phase of mediumship is still being given in many séance rooms all over the world today.

Undoubtedly, spiritual healing was the outstanding phase of the Master's mediumship and the New Testament is filled with instances of his marvellous healing power. We also have evidence that his disciples were too endowed with the gift of healing, especially Peter. The fact that these "greater works" that Jesus promised are still carried on can easily be proven, for our Spiritual Healers of today have performed marvellous cures and in many cases the medical doctors have declared the sickness incurable. How true are the words, "all things are possible with God" Today we are taught that we can be brought back into harmony with God through the psychic power of healing mediums but we also know that the person being healed must have faith in the power to heal and that the healing cannot be permanent unless we cease to break the law that originally caused it.

While the word Spiritualism was probably never used or even coined when the Bible was written, still the religion which we know as Spiritualism has played an important part in the life of man since the beginning of time. Even taking into consideration the fact that no book has ever gone through so many translations as has the Bible, and with the subsequent alterations which we know have been made, still in all the teachings of Jesus, those of us who look deeply enough can find the fundamental truth. That people have begun to question certain passages in the Bible is evident by the fact that within the past decade several translations have been made, the latest of which, accepted by most orthodox churches, was presented to the public just a few years ago.

The story of the crucifixion is well known – the capture of Jesus, the trial, the nailing to the cross, etc., the chief priests, the scribes and the elders mocked him as he hung on the cross. We can understand that these priests, scribes and elders of the church were as ignorant of the necessary conditions for the production of spirit phenomena as some few people of their profession appear to be today. The very air was full of murder and brute force ruled the day. There was no one spiritual there except the dear medium himself – Jesus, and he was beautifully spiritual, for he said:

"Father forgive them, for they know not what they do".

This was indeed spiritual, God bless him. Jesus suffered death at the hands of the priesthood, the elders of the church and the offices of the law, for the crime of teaching Spiritualism and demonstrating, through his mediumship, the truth of a life after death for mankind.

Here at his crucifixion we have evidence of a very dark séance and very powerful spirit phenomena, for Mathew writes "Now from the sixth hour there was darkness over all the land unto the ninth hour." "And about the ninth hour Jesus cried with a loud voice, saying "Eli, Eli lama sabachthani"? That is to say 'My God, my God, why hast Thou forsaken me'? "The temple was rent from top to bottom and the earth did quake and the rocks rent". Would you say that these were extremely powerful spirit manifestations?

Perhaps the most beautiful of all the stories are those of the materializations of Jesus. Jesus materialized 11 times including his ascension forty days after Easter. I will relate the story of my favourite – Early in the morning of the first day of the week, after the crucifixion, Mary Magdalene, Mary the mother of Jesus and some of the other women went to the sepulchre and found the stone rolled away. You will recall Mary Magdalene ran through the garden to find the Disciples and she saw a man walking in the Garden. Thinking that he was the gardener, she ran to him and saith – "Tell me where have they laid my Master" and then according to the Gospel of John:

> "Jesus saith unto her 'Mary.' She turned herself and saith unto him, "Rabboni". Which is to say Master? "Jesus saith unto her, "Touch me not; for I am not yet ascended unto my Father and your Father and to my God and your God".

This was the Master's first materialization after the crucifixion and it is quite evident that even he, who knew the law so well, could not materialize perfectly the first time, else Mary would have recognized him at once. Perhaps the gardener was also a medium. Does not this story answer much criticism of materialization – for it is true that a materialized spirit draws much of his or her power to materialize from the medium being used and often resembles the said medium; Also, we too are told not to touch the ectoplasmic figures.

Today we celebrate the first Sunday after Easter as Circa Prima – which is Latin for "1st Circle". This was Jesus's 6th materialization and is of particular interests to Spiritualists for this was the first Christian séance, when he appeared to his disciples. It had all the elements of a modern séance. It was scheduled, a true place was set, the doors and windows were locked – there was even a sceptic, Thomas. Thomas was with them on that Sunday evening after Easter and said "Except I shall see in his hands the print of the nails; and put my finger into the print of the nails, and thrust my hand into his side, I will not believe". The disciples were gathered together in the upper chamber, having locked the doors because of their fear of the authorities, when Jesus appeared amongst them saying to Thomas: "Reach hither thy finger and behold my hands and reach higher thy hand and thrust it into my side; and be not faithless but believing".

Today there are still many doubting Thomas's – those who must literally "feel the print of the nails" before they believe. How many times have we heard the spirit people say "Never doubt again that I live and can return to you:"

Surely these materializations furnish enough evidence that the so-called dead can return and manifest in an ectoplasmic replica of their former human body. There are those who believe that these appearances of Jesus were in a physical body and in fact he is quoted as saying in the Gospel of Luke "handle me and see; for a spirit hath not flesh and bones, as ye see me have".

Now of course Jesus knew that the disciples were terrified because he was a spirit and he had to reason with them in some way that he might instruct them as to the work they had to do. Many of you can testify to the fact that a materialized form has weight and can be solid and tangible to the touch as a physical body, yet it can disappear (dematerialize) just as Jesus did after he had broken bread with the two disciples at Emmaus.

Nature's law proves to us that flesh and blood cannot

enter into the heaven world, only the spirit and its spiritual body ascends into the world of higher vibration at the time of so-called death. Therefore, we do not believe that the physical body of Jesus made its ascension. We are also asked what then became of the physical body of Jesus. Possibly it was stolen and buried by those who loved him; however, it seems most logical to believe that he himself de-materialized it for the scriptures tell us in many instances of his knowledge of the laws of materialization and dematerialization of matter.

It is quite natural for us to believe that Jesus returned after his crucifixion to help the disciples to carry on his work. His teachings, based upon his mediumship, must be carried on if the truths that he taught were to persist down through the ages. In that upper chamber when he materialized he gave his chosen disciples their instructions as to how they should carry on the work. He told them not to leave Jerusalem but to wait until they should be "baptized with the Holy Ghost", which is the spirit of power or in other words, until they had developed their mediumship and they would be guided then as to their future conduct.

The Pentecostal Feast and the "speaking with tongues", was evidently the combined force of all the disciples and many different tongues were spoken, tongues that were unknown to the simple Galilean fishermen. If they were all of accord they were all in harmony and this condition of mental harmony is conducive of good results in any séance. Luke also speaks of a rushing of wings – "And there appeared unto them cloven tongues, like as of fire and it sat upon each of them".

The rushing wind and the spirit lights upon each of them are familiar to all who have attended séances. These are not miracles but are manifestations of a natural law with which we are familiar today, for I'm sure many of you know of instances where a foreign tongue is spoken through mediums who understand only the English language.

It is fitting to end this Chapter with Saul as no discourse on Spiritualism of the Bible would be complete without some reference to the mediumship of Saul, later know as Paul. The story of the conversion of Saul is a beautiful story. It began with his witnessing the stoning of Stephen, and he begged to be allowed to follow these Christians who were flouting the laws of the Temple Priests – to follow them and bring them back to Jerusalem for trial. It was on that sin-stained road to Damascus that he heard the voice out of the Heavens:

"And I fell onto the ground, and heard a voice saying unto me. Saul, Saul, why art thou persecutes thou me? And I answered, who art thou Lord? And he said unto me. "I am Jesus of Nazareth, whom thou persecutes.""

It is truly said that no one is as firm in their beliefs as those who have been converted to a religion – and this was the case with Paul. Paul was really the "salesman of Christianity" – for he went from province to province, city to city preaching of Jesus. To him belongs the credit for writing the first book or letter that was later to become a part of the New Testament. In fact, Paul wrote many letters to various churches which he had organized and these Epistles were later incorporated in the New Testament. Among the writings attributed to Paul we find some of our most valued references for the continuity of life and the communion of spirit. In his first letter to the Corinthians he says:

> "For I am determined not to known anything among you, save Jesus Christ and him crucified".

Paul did not express himself very well here – had he used the word resurrected – but he didn't, or at least the translators did not put it so. This no doubt led to a belief in the blood atonement or Vicarious Atonement that is a part of the creed of practically every Orthodox Church. Spiritualists believe that Jesus proved the continuity of life by returning after his crucifixion but Spiritualists do not believe that his blood was shed as reparation for the sins of humanity. However, in the same letter Paul makes a statement which finds its counterpart in our Spiritualist Churches of today, when he says:

> "And my speech and my preaching were not with enticing words of man's wisdom, but in demonstration of the spirit and of power".

Those words are very true, for many people come to church for the messages rather than for the sermon. Paul tells us plainly of the value of spiritual gifts. Many of the phrases of mediumship which we are familiar today are mentioned in his ancient letter to the church at Corinth. We read:

"Now concerning Spiritual gifts, brethren, I would
not have you ignorant".

He tells the Corinthians that there is a diversity of gifts
and he also adds that the manifestation of spirit is given
to every man for his own profits. This thought coincides
with that of our Spirit Teachers when they tell us that
every human soul has some phase of mediumship but
all do not possess the same phase.

Paul writes – "For to one is given by the Spirit
the word of Wisdom – (Inspirational speaking –
lectures inspired by the Master Teachers).

"To another the word of knowledge by the same
Spirit" – (Teachers of Philosophy)

"To another faith and to another the gifts of
healing by the same spirit" – (How wise of Paul to
combine faith and healing in one verse, for without
faith there can be little healing).

"To another the working of miracles" – (This
we interpret to mean the physical phase such as
trumpet, materialization, etc. These things may
appear as miracles to those who do not understand
them).

"To another prophecy" "To another the discerning
of Spirits" (Isn't that clairvoyance?)

Nowhere in the literature of Spiritualism can one

find a clearer explanation of the various phases of mediumship.

CHAPTER 5

THE DEAD SEA SCROLLS

No modern series of lessons on the Psychic Interpretation of the Bible would be complete without some reference to the Dead Sea Scrolls and the brilliant light they have shed on Christianity.

You may recall that these ancient religious documents were found in Trans-Jordan in 1947, in a cave near the Dead Sea. The results of their study confirm their authenticity and great influence on the established religious teachings of the past century. Many books have been written on these Scrolls and therefore I will not go into too much detail concerning their discovery.

About a half mile South of the Cave where the first Scrolls were found, lie the ruins of what Pliny the Elder, a great historian, said was an Essene Monastery. One of these Scrolls gave the prescribed rules of order for an Essene Community and authorities have come to the conclusion that these Scrolls were written in this Monastery, known as the Qumran. Archaeologists have unearthed enough of the Community to be able to draw a pretty good picture of the living conditions, housing, etc., even to an elaborate arrangement to ensure the supply of pure water.

One of the Scrolls contains the book of Isaiah in its entirety, the text being in Hebrew and is very similar to the book of Isaiah as it appears in the Bible. In one or more of the Scrolls there is reference to a Teacher of Righteousness. The discovery is important for when they can be truly translated they will revolutionize the approach to the beginnings of Christianity.

It has long been known, for instance, that Christianity is largely composed of elements absorbed from pagan religion in the Mediterranean area during the early centuries of its development. Even the Jewish Sabbath, which both Jewish and Gentile Christians at first observed on the seventh day, was given up in favour of the Mitharaic Sunday, the first day of the week.

When it became known that one of the Scrolls described the organization of a community with marked resemblances to the first Christian churches, and that another spoke of a Teacher of Righteousness who may have been the martyred founder of this community, the general public, at least the Bible-reading public, became interested, even if it was only a possibility that scripture had been found, written in Judea before the time of Jesus. The dating of the individual manuscripts and the relation of each to the others and of all of them to previously known scriptures, both Biblical and non-Biblical, is an area, of course, in which much work remains to be done.

What we know now, with a probability which, for all practical purposes, we may as well call certainty, is that a Sect known as the Essene Brotherhood existed in the centuries just before the emergence of Christianity which was organized in ways that suggest a relationship to the early Christian churches. Writers on this interesting subject claim that the Essenes were practicing the main principles, later ascribed to Jesus, for a century before he was born, and a century after his death. They were well known near the early home of John the Baptist, and it seems fairly certain that Jesus himself must have contacted them. Many students of religion, in fact, credit the Essenes with laying the foundations upon which Jesus built.

Here are some of the points of resemblance between Essenism and the teachings of Jesus:

Essenes objected to oaths: Jesus is quoted as saying "swear not at all". The Epistle of James adds: "swear not, neither by heaven, neither by the earth, neither by any other oath".

Essenes recognized the service of angels: Jesus also emphasized this.

Essenes despised luxury: Jesus rebuked luxury, indulgence and the deceitfulness of riches.

An Essene rule was not to possess more than one garment at a time. Jesus taught: "He that hath two coats, let him impart to him that hath none", and he instructed his disciples not to have two coats apiece.

Essenes ate at a common table: a meal was preceded by blessing and prayer and a hymn. The story of the Last Supper shows a similar practice.

Essenes held views on resurrection, heaven and hell (derived from pagan sources): Jesus taught the same.

Essenes emphasized obedience to authority: Jesus said, "Render unto Caesar the things that are Caesar's". And his followers enjoined servants to obey their masters.

Essene houses had a chamber or monasterium for prayer and meditation: Jesus taught: "When thou prayest, enter into thine inner chamber, and having shut thy door, pray to thy father, which is in secret".

All possession and earning of Essenes were held in common, and distributed according to need. The Book of Acts states that "all that believed were together, and had all things in common", and none of them said that "ought of the things which he possessed was his own".

These numerous identities or similarities are surely extremely significant, or at least suggestive. As also is the following quotation: "As soon as the Christian church was well established, historians ceased to mention the Essenes. We conclude that they had merged with the groups that took the name of Christians".

Since the date of the Scrolls, have been fixed with the limits which suggest their significance for Christian origins, and the relationship of the Scrolls to Qumran's community have been established in ways that make this community of special interest in forming our views of early Christianity, therefore, it is now appropriate that we learn something more about this Sect, to equip ourselves for understanding the fuller import of the new discoveries.

The Bible does not refer to the Essenes, however several historians do and it is interesting to note that they too differ. One historian states that there was no marriage, in fact no women in the Sect, another states that there were some families, but these families lived apart. All agree, however, that the Essenes were saintly people, consecrated people that they loved a "Communal" life; they had a common storehouse, common expenditures, common raiment's and common food, eaten together. Their lives were devoted to God. They taught immortality and gave prophecies.

Much of their time was spent in the study of minerals and herbs for healing purposes and they were known as the "Therapeuts" or "healers". Every member of their Sect had to have knowledge and understanding of the old Jewish Laws.

There are references to the training of a Messiah which many historians believe indicates that both John the Baptist and Jesus received their training with the Essenes. If this is true we can understand how many of the rites and tenets of the early Christians came from the Essenes and the Scrolls found in a cave near the Dead Sea seem to confirm this.

Many narratives by the patriarchs found in the Old Testament have long been regarded as merely pious tales until some more or less recent archaeological discoveries when they were unexpectedly transferred to the realm of history, the door into the historical world of the Old Testament was suddenly opened wide. To quote just a few incidents:

In Palestine, places and towns that are frequently mentioned in the Bible are being brought back once more into the light of day. They look exactly as the Bible described them and lie exactly where the Bible locates them. On ancient inscriptions and monuments scholars encounter more and more characters from Old and New Testaments. Contemporary reliefs depict people whom we have hitherto known only by name. Their features, their clothes, their armour take shape before our eyes. Colossal figures and sculptures show us the Hittites with their big noses; the slim, tall Philistines; the elegant Canaanite chiefs with their "chariots of iron", which struck terror into the hearts of the Israelites; the Kings of Mari, contemporary with Abraham, with their gentle smiles. During thousands of years that divide us from them, the Assyrian Kings have lost nothing of their fierce and forbidding appearance. The scholars have also awakened from its ancient slumber the notorious Babel with its legendary tower. In the Nile Delta, archaeologists have found the cities of Pithom and Raamses. They have laid bare strata that tell of the flames and destruction that accompanied the children of Israel on their conquering march into Canaan. In Gibeah they found Saul's mountain stronghold, the walls of which once echoed to the strains of David's harp. At Megiddo they came upon the vast stables of

King Solomon, who had "12,000 horsemen".

From the world of the New Testament reappeared the palatial edifices of King Herod; In the heart of Old Jerusalem the Pavement was discovered where Jesus stood before Pilate, as is mentioned in St. John's gospel. Assyriologists deciphered on the astronomical tables of the Babylonians, the exact dates on which the Star of Bethlehem was observed.

These breath-taking discoveries, whose significances it is impossible to grasp all at once, make it necessary for us to revise our views about the Bible. Many events that previously passed for pious tales must now be judged to be historical. Often the results of investigation correspond in detail with the Biblical narratives. They not only confirm but also illumine the historical situations out of which the Old Testament and the gospels grew. At the same time the changing fortunes of the ancient people of Israel are woven into a lively, colourful tapestry of daily life in the age in which they lived. They were also caught up in the political, cultural and economic disputes of the nations and empires that struggled for power in Mesopotamia and on the Nile, from which the inhabitants of the tiny buffer state of Palestine were never able to completely detach themselves for over two thousand years.

The opinion has been, and still is, widely held that the Bible is nothing but the story of man's salvation, a guarantee of the validity of their faith for Christians everywhere. At the same time it is a book about things that actually happened. Admittedly in this sense it has limitations, in that the Jewish people wrote their history in the light of their relationship to Yahweh which meant writing it from a point of view of their own national history. Nevertheless, the events themselves are historical facts and have been recorded with an accuracy that is nothing less than startling.

Thanks to the findings of the archaeologists, many of the Biblical narratives can be understood better now than ever before. There are, of course, the theological insights which can only be dealt with in terms of the Word of God. But as Professor Andre Parrot, the world-famous French archaeologist has said: "How can we understand the Word, unless we see it in its proper chronological, historical and geographical setting"? Until now, knowledge of these extraordinarily discoveries were confined to a small circle of experts.

No book in the whole of history of mankind has had such a revolutionary influence, has so decisively affected the development of the western world, or had such a worldwide effect as the "Book of Books", the Bible. Today, after two thousand years, it has been translated in 1120 languages and dialects and gives no sign of having exhausted its triumphal progress.

Exciting discoveries have resulted from careful examination of the combined results of scientific investigation along many different lines. In view of the overwhelming mass of authentic and well-attested evidence now available, something keeps hammering in our brains – this one sentence:

"The Bible is right after all!"

CHAPTER 6

LANGUAGE

It is illuminating and fascinating to study the birth and growth of words. The word "Christian", for instance, was first jeeringly applied to the followers of Jesus and rejected by them. It is derived from the Greek word "Christos", which had originally no reference to Jesus and was roughly an equivalent of the Hebrew word "Messiah". Palestine, surrounded by the great powers of the world, had been the cockpit of the nations. Out of this unending misery and despair there arose in the Jews a yearning, gradually crystalizing into hope, that, lacking all earthly help, some great heavenly messenger would come to free them from the Roman rule. It was this idea that first animated the disciples when they followed Jesus, but Jesus did not fulfil their hopes, at least not in the way they expected. To label his followers as "Christians" was to link them up with the Nationalist Jews and the enemies of Rome, so the followers resented being called Christians, because it aroused the suspicions of the Roman authorities. This suspicion was strengthened when they, both Jews and Gentiles, refused to bend the knee before the bust of Caesar; therefore, they were considered unpatriotic and were persecuted. Their leaders, men of great strength of character, urged them to be strong and of good courage and not to mind being called "Christian". Thus, the term Christian becomes elevated from a term of abuse to one of hope.

There has been a great deal of controversy in recent years concerning the original language of the Bible – one of the authorities is Dr. George Lamsa, a man who was born, reared and received his early education in that part of the world where Jesus lived. The people there have, since the beginning of time, spoken Aramaic and still do.

There are sceptics who do not believe such Biblical stories as that of Jonah and the great fish. But Dr. Lamsa says if these sceptics learned a little Aramaic they would know that "to be in a great fish" is an Aramaic idiom meaning "to be in great perplexity".

The books of the Old Testament found recently in a cave in Palestine are in Aramaic and unquestionably were written centuries before the Christian era. Apparently, the great stumbling block has been the gross mistranslations of the original text of the Bible from Aramaic to Hebrew of the Old Testament, and from Aramaic to Greek, to Latin, to modern languages of the New Testament. Webster's unabridged dictionary writes categorically that Aramaic was the language spoken by Jesus and his Disciples. How, then, could the New Testament have been written originally in Greek? The Master Jesus was speaking to Jews whose language had been Aramaic for centuries. Only the most educated Jews understood Greek.

The translators from Aramaic into Greek did not know the definition of the Aramaic words. It is evident too; that the translators of the King James Version did not know the fine shades of meaning conveyed by "Eloi, Eloi, Lama Sabachthani". They translated this phase as, "My God, my God why hast thou forsaken me"? Modern authorities, better versed in the language, give us the true meaning of "My God, My God, for this was I created". Confirming evidence for this translation is furnished in John 18:37 – While Jesus was before Pilate, on trial for his life, he declared, "To this end was I born and for this cause came I into the world".

One authority states: "this special value of the ancient Syriac (Aramaic) text is not mainly, in the fact that it proves these Gospels within 50 years of the apostolic age – no intelligent person doubts that now – but because it gives the version of the New Testament used in Palestine at that early age, being written in the Eastern branch of the very language which our Lord and the apostles spoke.

Dr George M. Lamsa, a native born Aramaean, who is thoroughly educated in the language Jesus spoke and is also an excellent English scholar, has translated the entire Bible, both the Old and the New Testament, from the original Aramaic into understandable English. Dr. Lamsa wrote: "My own struggle to master the often confusing idioms of the English language made me realize how the Bible has been mistranslated and misinterpreted by those early scholars".

In the book of Numbers we read – "And Moses lifted up his hand, and with his rod he smote the rock twice; and the water came out abundantly and the congregation drank and their beasts also". As the passage stands one might picture the prophet Moses as pounding on a rock with his staff. Dr. Lamsa clarifies this matter by stating that wells were very precious property to desert dwellers. After using all the water necessary, a large flat stone was placed over the wells to keep out beasts and sand. On returning to the spot later someone took a staff and sounded for the rocky well cover just as we today rap on house walls to find the location of the joists. The plain fact is that Moses sounded for the stone cover and having found it by the depth of his rod, penetrated the same, and ordered his people to dig away the sand.

The passage in 1 Kings, states "And it shall be, that thou shall drink of the brook; and I having commanded the ravens to feed thee there. "Great paintings hang in galleries showing Elijah being handed food by a flock of ravens. Once freed from Oriental mysticism the story is clarified and made believable, for the Aramaic word "erav" means ravens and it also means Arabs. The Arabs, not the ravens, fed Elijah. We are indebted to Dr. Lamsa for this logic and sensible interpretation.

Salt in the East is a symbol of barrenness. Dr. Lamsa explains that Lot's wife, who disobeyed God's command, was punished by being barren, instead of being turned to a pillar of salt. The Aramaic word "Araa" signified "earth" or "field" or "region". Dr Lamsa writes that the Genesis account of Noah and the flood is twisted into improbability because of the mistranslation of "araa".

He declares that the great flood covered only the region between the Tigris and Euphrates rivers.

Revelation states that any person who abstracts from or adds to "this book" is dammed forever. Revelation was written in Aramaic by John and was not made a part of Holy Writ for many centuries afterwards. Lamsa proves conclusively that Revelation was written in the language Jesus spoke and read. Dr. Lamsa being Aramaean correctly translates the book and points out that John was simply warning against forgeries: "Many Aramaic manuscripts of Holy Scriptures, liturgies and other sacred writings contain warnings against forgeries". Times innumerable he calls our attention to the fact that in translating Aramaic with its idioms, to Greek with its idioms, to Latin with its idioms and to English with its idioms, serious errors were made. To correct an error in translation is not forgery.

A final proof that mistakes occur in the translation of one language with its idioms into another language with its idioms is found in The Lord's Prayer. Consider the clause, "And lead us not into temptation". Common sense indicates that God does not tempt man into sin and crime. Jerome so translated the Greek text into the Latin Vulgate. However, Dr. Lamsa translates it direct from the Aramaic version, "And do not let us enter into temptation". This makes God a kind and beneficent friend who is willing to keep us out of trouble instead of leading us into it. It is interesting to note that in the Revised Standard Version of the Bible the word "medium" is used instead of "witch".

A few extracts showing Spiritualism in relation to the Bible:

Spiritual body – "There is a natural body and a spiritual body". 1 Cor: 15–44

Physical Manifestations – The angel unloosened Peter from chains in prison – "When they were passed the first and second ward, they come to the Iron Gate that leadeth into the city, which opened to them of its own accord and they went out". Acts: 12–10 an angel went before them in a cloud. Ex: 14–19. The moving of a table now is paralleled by an angel rolling back the stone from the door of the sepulchre. Math: 28–2.

Inspiration and Mediumship – "For to one is given by the spirit the word of wisdom; to another the word of knowledge by the same spirit". 1Cor: 12–8 "And the spirit entered into me when he spake unto me" Ezek: 2–2. "To whom hast thou uttered words, and whose spirit came from these?" Job: 26–4.

Speaking in Unknown Tongues – "To another divers kinds of tongues; to another the interpretation of tongues". 1 Cor: 12–10. "And they were filled with the Holy Ghost and began to speak with other tongues, as the spirit (which controlled them) gave them utterance" Acts: 2–4.

Materialization and Clairvoyant Appearances – An angel appeared to Hagar, Gen: 16; three came to Abraham so perfectly materialized, that "they did eat." Gen: 18 an angel appeared to Joseph in a dream,

Math: 1. an angel appeared to the two Marys at the sepulchre; to Zacharias. Luke: 1 to Mary, Luke: 1 to the shepherds. Samuel appeared "covered with a mantle". A spirit appeared to Daniel "clothed in linen, whose loins were girded with fine gold". Dan: 10. Feeding the multitude of 5,000 on five loaves and two fishes, Luke: 9 12–17 making wine at the marriage feast. John: 2 1–9 and lastly the several materializations of Christ after crucifixion.

Trance – "How he was caught up into Paradise and heard unspeakable words which it is not lawful for man to utter". 11Cor: 12–24. Like all those who have fallen into trance, he did not know "whether in the body or out of the body" "which saw the vision of the Almighty, falling into a trance, but having his eyes open". Num: 24–16.

Direct Spirit Writing – On the walls of Babylon: "In the same hour came forth fingers of a man's hand and wrote over against the candlestick upon the plaster of the wall of the King's palace, and the King saw the part of the hand that wrote". Dan: 5–5.

Levitation – This is clearly expressed in Ezek: 3–14 – "So the spirit lifted me up and took me away". And more explicit in 8–3, "And he put me forth the form of a hand and took me up between earth and heaven and brought me in the vision of God to Jerusalem 1 Kings: 18–12. Christ walked upon the sea, Mark: 6–49.

Clairvoyance – "Come see a man told me all things I ever did: Is not this the Christ's" John: 4–16 to 29.

Stephen Acts: 7 55–56. "Behold I see the heavens open and the son of God standing at the right hand of God".

Clairaudience – "And he fell to the earth and heard a voice saying unto him: Saul, why persecutes thou me? And the men which, journeyed with him stood speechless, hearing a voice, but seeing no man". Acts: 9 4–7; the apostles heard the voices of Mosses and Elias on the mount, Math: 17 3–5 also. Rev: 1–10 – The entire Book of Revelation is professedly the utterance of one in trance.

Healing – "They shall lay hands on the sick and they shall recover", Mark: 16–18. "And Jesus put forth his hand and touched him and immediately his leprosy was cleansed", Math: 8–3. Peter cures the lame man, Acts 3: 1–8. Jesus healed by magnetic touch, "And the whole multitude sought to touch him; for there went virtue out of him; and healed them all", Luke: 6–19. "Elisha restores the life of the Shunammite child" 11Kings: 4 33–35.

CHAPTER 7

AQUARIAN AGE

(The new age of spiritual development)

Rev. J G Tingley's class of 29th June 1968

Once again I am happy to instruct you, to serve and to reach out for renewed and fresh inspiration. I believe that the word "Inspiration" becomes a striking keynote to the new age we are definitely in.

Before going further take a moment to open your mind by entering the silence in a short period of meditation. In as much as possible, try to remove from your mind all the sensory conditions of the physical domain. Call in the response of Spirit. *This will relax the body, calm the mind and help you focus more on the lesson in hand.*

Dear students – We have entered the new age of spiritual development and the reaches of the soul powers. With the entering of this new age of psychic and physical action, we must concentrate upon the methods that are most applicable. We must stimulate our minds and we must stimulate our bodies at the same time. This is very difficult for the average individual, as they must first keenly attune to a sense of responsible duties that must take performance within the mind and the body and within the experiences of life.

The individual entering into the new age must take upon them a certain amount of responsibility. They must not only be aware of the nature of the incoming planetary expressions and the various happenings that are taking place now and going to take place, but they must do something about it. In sociology and human relations, we find that we are preparing ourselves for a better sense of living in the physical incarnation of life. We see modes of travel changing; we see new expressions of architecture; we see all the grand steps of progression that have been made in various fields of art and science. But I am especially interested in the inner nature of man: your mind, your relationship between mind and matter and your conscious state of understanding. Do understand that there is a great dynamo of change living within the sensory department of your being – known as the mind; where everything is pre-formed and created. Let us prepare ourselves with a new education and with the new education of the great Aquarian Age that is upon us. We must have a new form, so to speak; a change in orientation. We must reach out and give ourselves newness. For as I often said, we cannot put new wine, into old bottles! We must reach out from within in order to receive that which is going to manifest in the exterior reach of hands, body and any form of transcendental experience.

There is a great transcendent power that people of this physical plane are not aware of. They call themselves the intellectuals, and they are those who are entering the great academies of learning, (the academic students), are becoming the intellectual starvelings of the present generation. Why? Because they have gorged and filled their minds so full that they have lost the perceptiveness of soul development. They have gorged and filled their brain cells; yet, at the same time they have not received new orientation to the key of living. They have lost sight of soul-consciousness, that which reaches out and expresses itself in physical terms. The ancient master, The Christ, who was the greatest example of soul-power, left this query with the world' "For what would it profit a man if he gained the whole world, and lost his soul?"

Now we find ourselves caught up with a master statement of the Bible. "For what would it profit a man if he gained the whole world, and loses his own soul?" I believe this to be one of the greatest lessons taught by the ascending group, The White Brotherhood, when they entered the silence of the catacombs and developed soul receptivity. In this modern day, we enter the séance room for the development of soul consciousness. We are the benefactors of radio and television, benefactors of all the wonderful gadgets that pick up established vibrations that are around us and transmit their wonderful performances. Had we spoke of this prior to its early development, we would have received an immediate lunacy commission. Isn't that right? We would have been promptly ushered into a lunacy ward and institutionalized. Yet, today a person is able to appear, speak and be heard in your living room from all the remote corners of the world. What radio and television is to the human eyes and ears, psychic receptivity is to the nature of soul. These are the things I want to impart to you in this lesson:

1. The development of soul

2. The realization that soul power is psychic energy, that forceful power that is invested within the very consciousness of man, whether in human manifestation or some other form or aspect.

Now, I want to say, do you think that impressions that come to you are necessarily just imagination? When one is striving for the reach of soul development in the séance room, they must realize that one individual cannot minister anything to another person unless he has first ministered it unto himself. He must find the awareness, and be completely cognizant of everything that is happening before it is photographed upon the mind or the attention of whatever or whomever he/she may be coming in contact with. You cannot even feel an object until first you have recognized its presence in some mental sense of being. You would have to have knowledge of the source; you would have had to develop a psychical recollection and recognition of an object before it is touchable. He/she has to build the psychic energy up to a form of imagination.

Now, this subject of imagination in regard to the psychic world, at times, has manifested itself most dangerously to the individual. And they say, "Don't let your imagination sweep you into the orbs of something strange." I say, BALONEY! Imagination has psychical imprint. It is the first recognized facet of psychic unfoldment. Do not be afraid of it. But let me caution you. Control it with the understanding that it is form, a very definite form of psychic presence and psychic energy. Without imagination, the artist would be lost; the writer would be lost and the creative power of God would be lost as an indwellant factor in the consciousness of all minds. Imagination must be present and then it must be harnessed. I pray that you understand this. Remember that even in this new age you can find wonderful results from soul development. How can you disbelieve the authenticity of your own being, when your being is the very result of psychic law energy – manifested here in a physical body? To me, you would be like a puppet dangling upon a string if you did not have an inherent degree of psychic knowledge. And so I stress that already, you are alive in this new age with a newness of power. Whether you are using it or not is another thought and question. What I want you to do, is to tap this source and to feel the great vibrant force of Spirit moving, surging, permeating your consciousness and lifting you to a loftier expression of consciousness.

Society today, as a collective group, has lost its vision because it has not tapped its psychic roots and the rudiments of spirit itself. Society has only become absorbed in the saturations of the earth plane, and this is very dangerous to the mind. That is why our mental institutions are filled to capacity, because a lacking of spiritual perception and reaching out by the individual has not been initiated. The new age of Spiritualism and psychic development, however, teaches this.

We learn during the course of our spiritual unfoldment that we must be the "key that unlocks the box of keys". For you are the great master of your soul's development and you are going to be that one passage that is going to flow into the greater expression of individualism and collective embodiment of a better society in which to live; in which to demonstrate; in which peace, love, happiness and psychic illumination shall rule. A universal acceptance of this power must come about.

You and I, as individuals, shall become the forerunners of this great and beautiful era that we have entered into, where Spirit is beginning to do the magic that has been thought of as the impossible. I believe that we can harness the power of levitation and lift greater things than pyramids and the unknown qualities of life, together. We shall become the elasticity of the unknown, the glue of the vibrant source known as Universal Law. We shall become closer to its relationship and we shall develop these powers, like they should be developed. However, do not search for the puerile expression, but move into this with a perceptiveness, with the knowledge that, "you are going to reach the ultimate". I am not introducing you to cult, creed, secularism or any other image of the past. I am providing for you, that you can provide for yourselves the means and steps to unlock the séance room for yourself. One of the greatest Lyceum heads of the past was Andrew Jackson Davis who stated, "We can enter into the inner sanctum of our self and feel the condition which is present here and now". You must feel the special condition of the present age, this wonderful change over from the Piscean Age to the Aquarian Age. This change is not simply a change of moving one sector point into another degree of the Zodiac, but it is a re-vitalizing, rechargeable power that is going to sweep into the being of every citizen of earth.

You are going to be exactly what your thoughts are. You are going to be and live in a world of all men's thoughts in as much as the aggregation of thought power is concerned. So let these thoughts be sent upon the waves of ether as great beams of intellectuality, as the best of soul thoughts, as the best of soul consciousness and they will create and further create for you, that which is the goodness of society, the balance of society, the goodness of political relationships, one with another and social order will be upon the physical, astral and mental planes of life.

You are going to live in happiness only if you plant seeds of happiness within your thoughts. You are going to experience fruition and power; you will use these eternal verities only if you plant the seeds, till the soil and come into direct consciousness with yourself. Until then, you are going to be lost. Is it no wonder that the intellectual starveling of today, the man I call the academic student, is primarily stultifying his soul power. He is petrifying; he is causing his soul power to become a hardened mass which is incapable of becoming flexible and reaching out into one's being. This newness of thought is the pushing and doing away with the puerile expressions and forms of living that are so detrimental to our progression.

Now, we enter the séance room and the medium enters also; suddenly the forms appear – ethereal, solid or materialized. Is this a strange feat? Actually, it is the development of soul power functioning; the development of a latent power that rests within the individual, but more possible for those individuals who are organically in shape, fit in mind and able to execute this development. It must be understood that not all people can become materialized mediums. I think, basically, of when Jesus took Peter, James and John up the mountain to pray. To pray means to go and enter the silence as you and I have entered the silence of [meditation]. But yet, He conditioned himself. He reached out and felt His own condition by tapping upon the facets of the soul nature of being. He put into operation the thought that He must go away, that He must establish new conditions. He must get away. So I suggest to you, in your leisure hours, get away from the throng, the masses, perhaps not up a mountain, but in the secret passage of your own understanding and nearness or proximity thereof. Go into, get in tune with the higher vibrations and homogenize these thoughts and ideals. And I repeat, we are entering a new age, but we must have new orientation of thought; we must have new education to meet these wonderful things that are transpiring around and about us. With newness of education, we must have a newness of physical action and mental action ourselves. I call it courageous action. We have to have courageous action to take a mortal leap into this thing called living – life itself. This is not supernatural action, but a "Supernormal" happening inasmuch as usage is concerned. Never supernatural, for it is as natural as the breath we are breathing and as natural as the oxygen and other gasses that comprise the entire universe of earth and regions beyond this extremity of life.

I am also interested in your color vibrations of thought. Do not think of color only as an expression of dots of paint upon the easel, but think of color as living thoughts that you possess yourself. For every thought and every vibration of thought, has color. It is contingent upon the actual hue of your thoughts. You are exactly what your thoughts are. You will experience just what your thoughts are capable of manifesting for you. You may say, "What has happened to me? I cannot claim it. It is not my fault". Be very, very careful with your statements for oft times we do not know what beneficial law lies behind the scene of action or reaction. Isn't it true? And we often become escapist of our own doings. Whether we want to accept this or not is another matter. However, nine times out of ten, we will discover that we are responsible for much disorder in our lives – and oft times too much responsible. This is difficult to admit to one's self. But environment dictates it; the law of environment and the conditions round us. The Law of Attraction immediately comes to mind; for it is sweeping through the universe. Its immutable presence, attracting the forces of nature both physical and spiritual, is going to move you and condition you into betterment. Not only of understanding, but of the manifestations that you are and will be, in whatever path of life you move.

A short time ago, a student asked me about my use of

the term plateaus. Let us not make finales of too many plateaus in our thinking, because they are permanent stop offs in life. Let's build peaks rather than plateaus. For peaks reach higher; plateaus are often just drop off places where we linger too long. And not in the words of philosophy, for philosophy and religion have not made "Good Bedfellows". Philosophy and religion have not gotten along too well in the last century or two. I am prone to believe that when you speak of the philosophy of Spiritualism, you are more or less talking about its religious aspects, rather than the understanding and development of nature itself. So in your quest of Spiritualism's philosophy or the anatomy of occult science, be careful not to define it as only a religious aspect, but define it as the reaching and knowing of organic and the exterior form of thought itself. You may find yourself much farther ahead of the intellectual starveling and more knowledgeable as a sensate.

I know people who can stand upon the platforms, who can amass a powerhouse of vocabulary. This is marvellous. But they cannot comprehend the deep meaning of their words as far as applying the definitions correctly in their lives. Metaphysics for everyday living is essential. You may be the greatest metaphysician, dramatically speaking. You may be a wonderful teacher, but if you haven't got the brawn, the physical action to move in and use, you haven't got anything. You haven't got the perspectives of thought to know how to properly define the being of metaphysical action. You must use a method. And what is method? A method is not supposed to be defined; it's supposed to be refined into motion.

And the only way I can refine it into motion is to let it work as a means to measure the soul power. How much elasticity must it have? How much power does it bring to me? Does the reach of the mind do anything for this? I stand before the mirror each morning and view the countenance there before me. Is it I that I see? No! It is but that shell that I am living in. Is it the temporal home upon this physical plane that I inhabit!

"In the beginning, darkness was upon the face of the deep". This was the Genesis of Moses' teachings. I believe he wanted us to have a metaphysical enlightenment rather than just an historical origin. I believe the Genesis he wanted us to find was enlightenment. The power of understanding shows that all knowledge is light, all mysteries are light and all force of God's energy is light, accessible to our understanding. Then we can move into the illumination and out of the realm of darkness and therefore, develop.

A young child approached me recently and his mother asked, "Don't you think that children should stay away from the séance room?" I don't believe that's true. I believe if we had more children in properly conducted séances, and educated them as Andrew Jackson David suggested, they would mature with a proper knowledge of the laws of nature and be much better adults and citizens of the present era. Then I was asked, "Don't you think it's going to be a dangerous shock to their growth?" What an erroneous, negative approach! Just because you are mature individuals sitting in a class, it is not a proper assumption to declare you are grown up. Many of you have only grown older in physical stature.

I think that many of us live in what the circus people call "The Peanut Ring," and we don't know much of anything, least of all anything about the soul, spirit and the realities of life, truth and understanding. Please do not misunderstand me. I can become a medium and use this power yet receive nothing as far as soul development is concerned. It is direction of power that makes the difference. Remember, that you must move a vibration higher than this to develop and attain the eternal verities. Are you directing the power for positive goodness or negative goodness? Are you directing the power to soul development or earth development? Or are you the person who has stultified and limited the powers of the mind and soul? I know that genius and insanity are very close cousins. So BEWARE! Be accurate with your directions of physical energy and avoid compulsion at all cost.

Compulsion: That abominable force of wickedness that drives all men to the pits of his own hell. It rolls along the earth in rage; succumbing all life in its path. It wills its influence upon all life from the utmost expression to the lowest of the fallen angels. Beggar man to bigger man, the noble and the wise; all are potential victims of its reward, "Mundane Evilness". It swallows up the genius in the blinding brightness of the sun and devours the ignorant in the blackness of the night. I say "REPLUSION" not compulsion.

One may deny this advancement through the silent strength of your consciousness in the form of mind over matter as opposed to compulsive matter over mind. Positive volition is the greatest tool against the influenced of self-destruction. Infinite strength from the spiritual expression of life is mine, if only I call upon it. Call upon it through soul development; for soul is developed rather than just a counter part of natal inheritance. The soul must be fed spiritual food just as a body must receive food to sustain itself and grow. A man's soul is not a sprout of parentage but is his individual storehouse of sensitiveness which he must kindle and nurture. And what is this sensitiveness.

Sensitiveness is the basis of mediumship. It is this ability to attune one's vibration to the vibration of external influences. The ability to attune one's vibration to another vibration beyond the physical expression of life is called mediumship. The Law of Attraction governs the degree of sensitiveness according to the development of the state of mediumship. The ability to perceive any rate of vibration is sensitiveness.

I have touched upon many facets of spiritual growth. Each facet dovetails the other. This is progression! This is creation. Creation and progression are the constituents of life. They are electives of life governed by the individual's spiritual right of "Free Choice". You are free to develop your intellect and being to any degree of your choice. To progress is to maintain a constant elevation and improve your qualities. To create is to express and demonstrate your choice. I pray that your spiritual ambition is fulfilled and gorged with renewed and fresh inspiration.

CHAPTER 8

A FAITH FOR ALL SEASONS

Students this next piece requires imagination – imagine being one in an audience of several, sitting on pews shoulder to shoulder in a full to capacity church, eagerly awaiting the Reverend J G Tingley's Lenten address.

Reverend J G Tingley addressing his congregation

In this mass of many on that cold February evening, the energy levels must have been high, the expectations affording excitement to the privilege of being present, awaiting the words of an exceptional and knowledgeable medium but also a metaphysician, a master of his subject and in his day, unparalleled a spiritual teacher.

(Definition of Lent – A period of 40 days before Easter to remember the events leading up to and including the death of Jesus, so named after an old English word meaning 'lengthen' or longer days).

Lenten Presentation by Rev. J G Tingley: Toledo Ohio

Beloved Friends!

This evening, of course, we recognize the beginning of the great Lenten period; that period of time when we look into the life of the Master Teacher (Jesus) and all the initiates who have come into this physical world to show us a sign, a light, and to bring us a message of spiritual intelligence. I am not going to bore you with extraction from the biblical literature, because we should be fully aware of the stories and miracles which have been brought to our attention regarding the consciousness of the great disciple; one who came to us in this physical form, the expression of infinite intelligence.

I want to speak to you about the conditions of the world today as we prepare to enter this Lenten period and bring forth the atonement of Spirit. In this world, it is most necessary for us to become conscious of a functioning power which lies within the individual. Let us look in a moment of retrospection to the great religions of the world and try to discover what they have done to promote this great initiate and bring to you and to me the consciousness of immortality.

First of all, immortality begins in this physical form of life as we so-journ. It is in the depth of every living expression and the depth of every being. I wonder if we can make an analysis and extract the part you and I play in the great role of this physical life. We have the great religions in our mists. You have and I have been members of other faiths. But we have now found a faith like Dr. Marcus Bach said, "Let that faith so permeate within our consciousness that it functions and moulds a great creative intelligence". Have we found this faith? Have we received the message of the great disciples? And especially at this time, are we prepared, are we making the proper preparation for our spiritual evolvement: I feel that we have not. For now when we come to make an analysis of retrospection, we can truly query the condition of the world's great religions.

I feel that the ethics and theology of the average church today is challenged. I feel that they are inadequate. I feel that they are not dispensing the message of the great disciple who came into our world and to show us the way of spiritual and physical living. We have missed the call of Spirit. If the great religions of today are inadequate, what is the answer? I say, the truest answer that I know and can give is my recognition of the spiritual potential which lies within the individual himself. In no other great church or religion, other than

Spiritualism, is there assurance of spiritual evolvement.

When I speak of Spiritualism, I want you to clearly understand. I want to say Spiritualism – Christian faith for those who believe not only in the continuity of life after physical change called death, but faith for those who believe in a religion that does for the individual what the individual cannot do for himself. What am I talking about? I am talking about the message of this great disciple (Jesus), the Master Initiate and the intermediary degrees of His wisdom. He opened up new channels for you and me and for all posterity, He said, "Listen unto the consciousness and the awaking of Spirit".

This was the vital message of the Master Teacher, and this is the message of Spiritualism. So I say this evening, while entering the Lenten period, let first be conscious, and then being conscious, we will readily discern the marvellous manifestations of the Spirit that can take place. In what matter and form will these transformations take? They will take the form of the absolute. How many of us sitting here this evening do not want to take an active part in life? We must be a part of life. We must be a participant. If we are not, then life does not give to you and to me it's real meaning and its real unfoldment. I say this as a Spiritualist. Because I feel that inherently, there lies within the domain of every living creature, that absolute potential of the spirit; that potential which the Master Teacher unveiled for us. The Lenten period should be a preparing school of the soul. It should be a preparing school to awakening our senses for the new age.

We are entering a great spiritual age; a great spiritual renaissance, which is the awakening of soul power and the complete knowledge of immortality. You are going to see in the next decade, marvellous strides in metaphysical methods and you are going to see people become more psychic then they have ever been before. Why? Because, it is inevitable, for the manifestation of Spirit has come. No longer is the day when people shall scoff at us and say all manner of evil against Spirit return and Spirit consciousness. For today, not only in the Spiritualist church, but in all other faiths, religionists are incorporating moments of silence and steps that certainly are very parallel to the Spiritualists who have practiced this throughout the years. And I say to you, wonderful! I am glad to see it, but it is about time as we say in the physical expression. It is about time!

Now, let us direct our attention, for a few moments, to the book of Jude, the first and the tenth verse, and hear these words spoken "And there are those who will scoff at us because they do not understand". I want to say that the first thing you want to aware yourself of is your own individuality. If first you understand and assimilate this vital truth mentally and spiritually, then you will see the transformation that I introduced in the epoch of my discourse this evening. Let us first prepare the consciousness and awaken this great and spiritual evolvement. There will be manifestations that come to each one of us that should have come long before this particular time. But what has happened. You have allowed your faith to be handled by the magistrates of learning, whose duty; you thought it was to concern themselves with such practices. Your ministers, your priests, your rabbi's, your great counsellors of faith; you have placed it all in their hands.

Now here comes the Spiritualist who says you have access to the vital potencies of this faith. You have access to these eternal verities. And I stress very emphatically; you have the manifestation of Spirit. If I may quote from the disciple Paul's wonderful letters, he said, "The manifestation of the Spirit is given to every man to profit with all". And so concern yourself in this Lenten period with the manifestation of the Spirit. But what shall I manifest first? I shall manifest my being. I will be and then I will be, aware. And if I am aware, I certainly will be sensitive to the vibrations of the great cosmic world of truth.

There is great transcendent power that evades the vast universe. And this power, as the Master Teacher said, is not limited to the access of just a very few, but to and for you and myself. If we are to be agnostic in our faith, then we will scoff the doubting Thomas's, of the day. If we want to become one who is very learned, so then will it be; but yet as learned as one may become, we can still fall into the practice of transferring guilt. I say transferring of guilt is when we allow these spiritual matters to become the property of only mediums, the property of only the advocate whose business it is to deal with these things. If we allow this to happen, there is nothing in the power vested within me that can save you. I can become an instrument between the two forms of consciousness and I can convey to you the beautiful messages of spirit. I can minister unto you to the best of my ability and in all humbleness; I can offer you the truth. But, unless the truth reaches you, all these efforts have been in vain.

Now, you do not have to become a supposed Spiritualist. But as I have repeatedly said to you, and I quote Lincoln's great words, "How can I be a religionist if I am not a Spiritualist"? And by being a Spiritualist, it is not only communicating with the so-called dead, it is communicating with yourself: The first key to the scriptures says that open doors shall be in front of us; the awareness of communicating with the great expression of spiritual intelligence. May this be very penetrable in your mind for this Lenten season does, especially, bring this to light more brilliantly than ever before! There is an unseen expression to behold, but actually my prayer this evening is a form of communication between you and me. If in this form of communication I can vitalize and charge the latent expression that is within you, then I am happy. If I can help you to communicate with yourself, then I have shown you the greatest lesson I could ever wish for. For it is not only communication with yourself and achieving understanding that there is life here and life beyond: it will help you to communicate with your everyday problems of life. In no other religion that I know is this knowledge revealed. I myself communicate in this way – I try to cope with it, not necessarily accepting it as the man in vain would say, "Oh! Accept it because you can't do anything about it ". I would not insult your intelligence by standing here telling you to accept things just as they are. Absolutely not! I do not want you to accept anything that does not belong to you – wealth, health, help or happiness, for sometimes happiness comes in disguise. Sometimes health is transformed into ignorance. So do not accept them, but violently express to yourself through metaphysical methods, through exercises of silent prayer, through communication between the finite and infinite expression, to deal and cope with today's problems with understanding. We do not have to hold and clench them in our hands. That is why hands are so loose that they can release and let go.

To enlighten you about the manifestation of the inter-consciousness, I want to say that present day religion, as far as the universal great religions are concerned, is doomed, because their ethics and their very theology is challenged. It is challenged by the plight that we see displayed around us. We see more mental hospitals today than we have ever seen before. In fact, there is very little room in those inns for the people already there. Why? Now I am a practitioner of faith and an advocate of truth so I say, had we received the great cosmic intelligence and the universal intelligence of the Master Teacher, had we had a preparation school within our sanctum, we would have escaped these conditions of illness that are so prevalent among us. Had we seen the light of consciousness, then illness would not have been so contagious or so anointed to our being.

Listen to that still small voice of Spirit. Listen tonight; I listen to mine, for never is there a day that I do not cling to the Infinite or come into the inter-sanctum with Spirit. Awaken yourself, for this universal plight is existent in illness both mental and spiritual because human beings do not know how to function. To function is to live. The Spiritualist Church says, "Let us function as a body of embodied truth". And I say, when we have done this, then we will not see the retardation that we see, the spirituality and mentally unequipped.

Tune into the psyche which is soul power. Tune in with the expression of the soul which is your only evidence of personal identity and the only part of you that is going to continue on after the change called death. You may be surprised, but the most brilliant of minds in our scholastic world are going to find themselves in a great human and spiritual dilemma when they make their transition. As highly degreed as they are, they will have a lot of unlearning to do.

Have you developed spiritually? Have you prepared yourself? Are you fit and able to come into this great Aquarian Age? Are you qualified? Think over these queries. They will afford their own answers. I am going to ask you to open your eyes and see the beautiful things that Spirit has to offer you; to open your eyes and see a new indentation of psychic phenomena, of metaphysics, of Spiritualism. I am asking you to give yourself a chance. To know that you are a spirit, living in the mortal, but you are not mortal. I am asking you to open the portals to education and development of self.

You have developed everything except you. You have amassed the money's of the world. You have manifested yourself in states and empires. You have kindled your fires and kept your hearth warm physically. But you are cold and fearsome inside, because that spark of divinity that illuminates has not been touched. So let us enter into this beautiful Lenten period spiritually and mentally. Aware yourself of the fact, that regardless of your status in the physical, you are an important being.

Every ounce of a palm will have its balance. Every measure of strength will have its usage. Every part of you will become charged with realization. There will be new frontiers for everyone regardless of the lowest status or the highest empire. A rolling away of the stone is the future. Neither depth nor height can measure the possibilities of the soul, but you can!

THE RED SEA

"When you come to the Red Sea place in your life,

And in spite of all you can do,

There is no way around; there is no way back;

There is no other way but through

Then know God with a soul serene,

And the night and the storm will be gone,

God stills the waves, God stills the storm,

God says to you, go on, go on, go on".

Anon

Christmas Eve 1970 – Rev. J G Tingley's address to his congregation

Upon this beautiful Christmas Eve, I would have you to take vision of the Master tonight, the vision that was perhaps imprisoned within the minds of many disciples before the advent of Jesus the Christ. Tonight, just for a brief moment, let there be that holy stillness of spirit, vested within the consciousness of all mankind. Should we forget the message of Christmas? Should we forget that great inaudible song that sung in the mentality of mankind prior to this evening – a majestic quietude that reaches out further than all the consciousness of mankind?

We could speak in the terms of metaphysics. We could speak in the language of theologians. We could raise our voices to a Bryant or a Tennyson and we could master the words of a grammar that would exalt the spirit of this mighty occasion. But still within the consciousness there is that "Knock", the spirit of a Holy calm that should instil the vestments of spirit, like the quietude that apparelled the world on this mighty occasion. When in the stars, there appeared a greater likeness to their nature and in the atmosphere of the great day of His coming, there appeared a scintillation that was far greater than all the illumination of the incandescence of this world of manufactured fabrics.

But yet, what was the real glow and what was the real silence that took place in this majestic silence? It was a silence that can only be known by the soul of a true psychic. The silence that was known only to someone who could peer into the dimly lit aisles of the past and not stand on the street corners of doubt. Someone who could look into the heavens and say "I believe not, that only once, that miracle of happening, takes place in this great silence of life." That likeness and that great brilliancy of spirit must manifest in the consciousness of reality. And this was actually what took place, for from the bed of Joseph came a dream when he, before the birth of his son, was to bring forth this message – "Low an angel stands beside me." An angel, one who has passed from the physical and vaulted walls of materialism, through the power of infinite intelligence, whispered into the audible sense of Joseph and told him about the great son that was to be born in Bethlehem and that he was to make the journey to the sacred city and the holy birthplace of our Lord and Saviour. It was a great clairaudient experience that he had, for in the stillness of the night comes that visiting one, like the poem which reads:

"Who knows who spoke to Joseph that very night?
And said, thou shall bring forth upon this creation
One who should instil our hearts with faith and
light."

This was a clairaudient message by way of a dream as the great biblical story relates. And as the theologians have mastered their pens, from their quills, we read these immortal words:

"Upon the face and consciousness of this earth
Emmanuel

And that great voice of the spirit of Christ shall ring".

Yet, there in the stillness of that night, stolen away from the mass and the pulchritude of all literature, we read the script well in our mind, for written is the message of communion before the time of Christ.

Now the bells have sounded low – now the star has moved gently – gently sweeping the orbs of heaven, leading the eyes of men that are desert bound, but fixed upon that one illumination. For in their breast they have another message. It is true that the angel did speak to the great spiritual man Joseph. It is true that in the quietude a marvellous experience happened and he was led by the dictates of spirit. It is true that communion was set forth, that men do not die but they rise to the majesty of the sweep of their own vision by tuning in with the expression of infinite intelligence. Moses adhered to these messages and then Moses swept his orb through the voice of Joseph, a quiet and just man. Why do I refer to Moses of old? It was in the time of Moses, from Genesis to Revelations that we heard of the coming, of this great man. Look into the silence and move with every moment of your breath into the passion of the new born King who has expressed the continuity of life and fill your mind with the same vision that Joseph had to fill his mind, though he knew the terror and peril that existed before him. He was led by the guiding light of an angel, of a spirit in ectoplasmic robes who led him further into safety to the manger where there should be born that day in Bethlehem the crown of all beauty and expression of life.

The great Christ message of the symbol is within our hearts this night. We feel that movement and we feel that passion of spirit – "Upon this day there is born in the City of David a child:" One that shall be possessed with the great beauties of life.

Awaken, fellow Christians, to the message of this age. For Christ must be born within our consciousness in the very same manner that He was born into the consciousness of those disciples who followed the gleaming star and who pierced the darkness that periled them from all the visions of materiality. Today, the real Christmas message should be a message not only of imagination, but it should have some kind of a realizing power within its constituents. The constituents of that message must read "vision born of action". Vision borne of great surety is a necessary form that leads man, when he is in stillness and in a tranquil spirit, to a manger of hope. This great story given, through the message of advent, is not to be confined to the dialects of the past, nor should it be robbed of the real beauty of understanding, for Spiritualism awakens it, so that we see the continuity of the star. We see that star far above all other stars in the heavens because it is a symbol. It is a symbol that inspires man. It is a symbol that makes man come closer to a realization of the infinite expression of intelligence. It is a symbol that has led him through the ages from the lowly vaulted walls of fear. From the dungeons that he has been incarcerated therein and from all the times and the fears that he has met upon life's way, that the same vision through the symbol must read in that same form that Joseph read the clairaudient message.

"Have peace my child, for thou shalt go into the City of David".

Have peace my friends for though we are saturated with much grossness of this physical world, we need a great renaissance of the soul. We need a similar renaissance of the soul that took place at that particular time when Christ was born in Bethlehem. We have to have light. We must have that light so bright and so clear to dispel the gloom that impoverishes us of the vision that is so necessary in this physical incarnation of life. And when can this miracle, so to speak, happen? Miracle I use, though it is inappropriate to the occasion, but yet necessary. It is necessary because it has vitalizing power within the consciousness of man when we come to the 20th century cradle of understanding – and we must know that vision is born of the inner soul and when the inner soul awakens to the consciousness of new birth, new birth can light the world with truth. No longer shall we be in the shadow of totalitarianism; no longer shall we be in the shadow of death that impoverishes us of the right of living. For in the message of the birth of Christ not only a Messiah had come, but a new order had come, a new reign, a new dispensation.

"And the angels shall send forth their harps
And they shall play upon the strings exalting His Spirit".

These were the words of the great transcription that are taken not only from the 'King James' version, but also from the other great bibles that have brought knowledge to us. They are epistles that are drawn from the Apocrypha, the hidden and the secret message of mysticism. For I know that prior to the time of Christ, that learned men stole away. They stole away into the secret counsel of silence. And while they were en-rapport with the vibration of God, messages came from the angel world. This is not a doctrine of supernaturalism; this is a message of truth. They stole away to find peace and to find great communion with the world that was not finite, in expression, but a world that was infinite in expression. And they knew of this great medium that was to come. John the Baptist knew. As a medium and through his instrumentality he said:

> "And one shall come before me and after me proving this great truth and I shall be His great, great voice of reverence and I shall prove to you that the star shall so shine that all the world shall be illuminated."

That star has dimmed only slightly. The only dimension of dimness that I can actually speak of tonight is the dimness that we allow to permeate our consciousness. The star shines bright in the heavens. It reaches out with all the brilliancy that it was given by the form of infinite intelligence. But for the lack of a receptacle to hold the brilliancy of its incandescent power, our minds have dimmed it by our own ignorance – the ignorance that we place there through not opening wide the portals of understanding. And that is why it is my earnest prayer; it is my sincere hope and wish, that in the ensuing days that are forthcoming and in the ensuing months that echo forth again, there will take place a response of the inner man.

This is not a doctrine of new thought, but it is a message of hope, a message that was known to the initiates and to the intermediaries and to the disciples of the white brotherhood before this child was born. This is a message of great spiritual understanding that was known by the men who were wise enough to open their minds to truth and to reach to a greater expression of the infinite intelligence. And this message friend has been cradled in a different form today. Cradled not in the form of reality, but cradled in the form of ignorance. We worship and follow a star that is only superimposed like circumspection of light that dimly pierces the dark and then is swallowed up by the engulfing gloom apparelled around it. This is a message of dimness that I see. For in the bulb that glows and shines and has scintillating value, there is still loss. That loss is that we see it through the naked eye of the individual.

Is there light enough in your eye to see the gleaming star tonight? Is there hope enough in your breast to receive the message that there is no death? Is there vitality and strength enough in your heart to walk the many miles of faith and discard the outworn dogmatic teachings that harass us and peril us from receiving the great message of the new born spiritual truth? Yes! I think this is the great state of apathy that has come into the world today – ignorance. We can boast about our great strength, about the wonderful creative powers of man: how he has created the vast beauties of this world, which is admissible and for which we should laud the creative intelligence, yet with all the grandeur of acoustics that we see and all the wonderful, marvellous civilization that mounts upon mounts and brings forth its great radiance through creation – that light that so led the wise-men has not come into the illumination of our soul consciousness. I say to you, I am happy to be a metaphysician. I am happy to reach out in Christian faith to know that transplanting the glory of that light of hope and the wisdom of the Masters must only come when I touch it.

Cradled deep within the vault of my daily ambition I must reach to a greater vault of this: Far out, but yet so near within is His eternal birth. Cradled only for those who wish to bow and pray for just a moment.

Call unto this great Christmas message of hope, for vested within here are our only symbols. And we are going to be led by symbol, even though not too long ago I read these words by a mighty minister, I say mighty as far as the universe of earth is concerned:

"Oh a wicked and perverse generation shall look for a sign in the skies. They shall be dismayed".

But I know that, that sign in the sky is going to be continued by other signs in the sky. I know that the star that led the wise-men to Bethlehem has multiplied with great, great stars that have flowed and flooded the atmosphere of thought consciousness in ways too numerable to mention. Be wise-men friends, is my message. Be wise-men to the secret of the silence. Be wise enough to follow the inner hope expression – be wise enough friends to open the epistles and read, "This day thou send thy son to be born in Bethlehem". And know that within your consciousness He is born. There is so much more that is above the Christmas tree than there is ever beneath it. For these things shall fade away in tinsel wrapped in yellow; they shall fade and to the ages they shall become known only. But that which shines, that is not seen by the naked eye; that inner response, shall be tinsel glowed through the ages with an eternal flame and a vibrant message.

I know that the music that I heard this evening was filled with the breath if His message. But not only was it the breath of the message of His coming and the advent of His being, but within the heart and soul of the musicians here, there had to be a voice. Was it similar to the one that stole into the eve of night and spoke to Joseph? Was it a star voice? Was it a voice of life?

A new dispensation of God is upon us. I do not have a message of Hell, Fire and Brimstone for you this evening. I have a message of light, and of truth. I have a message for a world of education. I have a message that we are all disciples following somewhere in the desert sands of time, but marked upon the breath of our experiences comes a winding, sweeping orb like a mighty clariant that blasts forth the message that Christ is suddenly alive. Do you know that He walks with you? And He talks with you. The very image of that tree unfolds His arms and reaches. I can see one of His first expressions after the great birth. Always carve and cut wood by the grain. How many of you Christians and theologians caught the message of Joseph in the workshop with his son. "Cut the wood by the grain". This had an inductive message of why He came.

1947, yes! A few years back, there the wondering sheep boy, somewhere along the black sea, just by chance, found an opening cave. The Apocrypha is revealed. The mystic magic of Christ is revealed. Suddenly, scrolls are revealed and now in this Christmas of 1970, it is permissible to say less than a decade away I see a light, a greater light of psychic consciousness coming to the world. This light, this beautiful light, which I introduce to you tonight is you, you are the light. The candle ever built in. And He lit the Truth.

And so friends, the bells receive a more expression now.
The scintillating candle glows and here upon us tonight
the angels sing once more.

   "There is no death.
   The stars go down to rise again upon a fair shore
   And brighten heaven's jewelled crown
   They shine forever more"

May this Christmas be the happiest and a most
prosperous New Year ahead is thine: Amen

MEDIUMSHIP: OUR HERITAGE

PART 3

VOICES OF WORTH

Into The Séance Room

The main spirit speakers during Reverent J. G. Tingley's trumpet, direct voice and materialisation séances were – Mable, Dr. Taylor, North Wind, White Feather and three children Jenny (epithet Snow White), Tulip and Lotus Blossom.

The following short extracts taken during séances conducted by Rev. James Garfield Tingley were recorded in 1989 in the presence of Rev. Ann Hart and Rev. John C Lilek. These passages formed the basis of teaching sessions. Although given to help those present at the time, the expressions still carry useful guidance for today's students of mediumship. I have simply used the excerpts given by the spirits Mable and Dr. Taylor as their voices were the clearest through the trumpet during the séances, plus given the age of the cassette recordings. The remainder of the cassette recordings containing general conversations between the sitters and their spirit guides, family and friends, are being donated (by kind permission of Greta Lilek) to the Holme Hall Healing and Spiritual Centre, Yorkshire England, for students who are interested in trumpet and direct voice phenomenon to hear and learn from. It is to be remembered that Christian Spiritualism through the means of the séance room does not need to be defended as it stands on its own merit! A communion through séance with the spiritual world is one of love, peace and knowledge and should never be derided. It is an opening to the higher energy realms and vibrations bringing us closer to God – the Supreme Spirit. To listen to these cassette recordings of voices from the spirit world is an education in itself and shows the remarkability of a dedicated, talented and gifted medium and the privilege granted to the sitters attending.

<div align="center">~~~</div>

Evening Trumpet Séance Extract – 29/09/1989

Spirit Mable Speaking:

"Hello dear children, isn't it so wonderful to be here once again, coming from out of the spiritual world – oh my dear children the spirit world is so close to you and so close to you when you remember the Lord.

I advise you children to set aside each Sunday evening to raise a state of spiritual awareness. Spiritual awareness is when the mind of the individual reaches beyond the five physical senses. You upon the physical plane of life must know that there is an infinite amount of power beyond the physical plane. All your life as I have looked through the archaic records, I have found that your innermost soul has desired a greater reach of intelligence and you have desired communication with the beyond, even before you were exposed to it. It is very very necessary for you to know and for me to teach you that in this series of wonderful training, that you will be tempted at times by those on the physical plan who have become negative towards such things. And so may I teach you in this lesson that spiritual awareness is always accompanied by negative vibrations of the earth world – the earth energy forces commonly known as people, people who don't understand the truth of the great Spiritual Being. And knowing this my children I had the same experiences when I was upon the earth plane but I was a very strong person and had a very noble and loving mother who had been in the work of mediumship for many years before and that was a great help to me. But being without that sort of background you will have many, many experiences of people trying to pull you down. You must overcome this yourself and once you develop the strong power of overcoming it yourself, you will have willpower and have a right to believe in your own concept of God. Every individual is an individual because they differ one from another. My lessons come to you from your individual willpower.

Will yourself, demand yourself to overcome all striking remarks against communication between the two worlds. This will seems a little strange to you and the best way to overcome it is by just walking away from the scene or conversation. Not indulging in a scene or conversation where there is bigotry and denial.

You can talk to some people endlessly with the greatest truth in your mind that the world will ever have, yet you will get nowhere with a closed mind. So you will face many closed minds in your experience of life.

Don't let this disturb you. It is perhaps one of the great hardships in developing true mediumship. Now Jesus the great teacher while he was on the physical plane taught discipleship. Discipleship comes from the word discplanation, to discipline oneself to a higher rate of vibration. And in this higher rate of vibration one finds that as we go higher and higher into spiritual awareness we are going to find the lower forces trying to pull us back down, it is not going to be an easy road. You are going to see the many strange ways that people will try and pull you down and strange experiences will happen to try to pull you down, don't allow it to the best of your ability. Use that strength of God. I will give you a little passage that helped me when on the earth plane: *Oh Lord let me be the master of my own fate.*

When you are master of your own fate then you are in control. Never be gullible. You are going to run into those super, colossal, so-called, would be mediums that are really not developed. Pay them no attention as one does not need to be around someone of that nature. It would not take long before you become aware of how little they know about the real subject.

And so you will be able to use what the Master Teacher Jesus said when He walked across the physical planes – He said I am able to separate the wheat from the chaff. There is a lesson itself in that. Be able to sort out the good kernels from the poor germs of wheat. So I say just walk away from public denial and public criticism and be the master of your own fate.

Open wide the portals of heaven in your thinking

capacity, there may come into your life, in your time and in your daily walk of life many material problems, conditions and thoughts. Sometimes to each and every person there are times of negativity that creep into the thought or the world of thought consciousness but you are taught only to reject them, not to claim them or take claim upon them. No man is perfect, except the Master Teacher.

Now I want you to visualise for a moment that you are in a very sacred console here in this séance room tonight. I want you to visualise yourself as going forward, to visualise the white light of Christ and a great and beautiful victory at the end of your accomplishments. A great and wonderful unfold that of developing mediumship. Hold this in your mind my children. Let not the angry passions of temper, disgust and worry interfere with your continuing on with this great and wonderful thing that is going to make you very happy. At the end of the road is a very happy person that you are going to create for yourself. It will take a little time but this is always the situation. The mighty oak grew from a small acorn, always think of this and envisage that little acorn but don't forget that it has to have the right conditions to enable it to grow. The conditions of mediumship that I am teaching you now are patience, concentration and control of temperament. We realise that you are living in a material word and have risen to a higher state of consciousness. We realise that you have problems that we do not have so we will be very patient with you. We realise that it is not easy to just turn the pages of life over to a newness that you never knew before. Mediumship is there; the powers that were asleep within you are there. You are awakening them gradually and so be proud of your advancement. Do not be content with just one mile, go all the way!"

~~~

Evening Séance 17/09/1989

Spirit Voice of Mable:

"I ask the Divine Spirit of God, to bring unto you the peace of mind that you might develop this wonderful gift of mediumship. To use your mediumship for the betterment of mankind and for the helping agent of goodness. Discourage gossip and slander. Do not be blasphemous unto the Lord God Almighty. Try to the best of your ability not to become discouraged or be a turncoat but pledge your allegiance to God and your spirit guides. Do not listen to those, whosoever they may be, that do not believe in the continuity of life and the communication between heaven and earth. For, you are a perfect child of God, and desire only the highest teachings of God and that which is noble, truthful and good. Obey the laws of nature both physical and spiritual and live in the valley of happiness to the best of your ability. This is my prayer for you".

Tonight's lesson children, is:
The Law of Concentration

"Concentration is the key to mediumship. It is the ability to focus one's mind upon a central object. That object should be chosen by the thinking capacity of the mind. Think of something very beautiful or something
~~~

that is pleasing onto your senses. Perhaps a beautiful scene of an ocean or perhaps of a landscape or the Master Christ walking upon the water or anything that is pleasing unto you. Choose anything you wish as I only give these as an example. Concentration is there in your everyday work but concentration is a little different in the spirituality connection, because you are concentrating upon the high potential. You are concentrating upon a higher level of spirituality. Rid yourself of all negative thoughts and enter into an elevation that is higher, higher and higher, slowly but surely all the disturbances of the day will leave. You will feel peace and a sensation of being whole. You will feel the spirit forces soothing your thinking capacity and feel the riddance of all disturbing factors that have crowded in during the day. Try to the best of your ability not to entertain any sinister force or sinister thought or any negative condition. Focus your mind upon the light of your object. The scenery that you have chosen to focus your attention upon, will enter your vision, it will embed itself in the deep consciousness of yourself and will act as a healing balm. It will be a part of you and being a part of you will allow progression to happen. One step at a time, but always forward, let this be your motto. This is what you will gain by true concentration. You will be able to use your concentrated power not only in gaining mediumship but in your everyday affairs.

The law of concentration plays a very important role so use it to meditate. Don't try to strain your brain as this is not true concentration. Don't try to commit to memory large amounts of data, it is not necessary. For what we are doing is opening your spiritual centres, we are causing the wheels to spin, which are called the chakras – this word comes from an old Sanskrit philosophy. In the great philosophy of the Sanskrit the Essenes and the Masters learned the laws of harmony and how to produce a contact to God. Concentration and the usage of physical powers must be attuned to God. Too many of your people upon the earth plane may be a little psychic but they failed to attune it to God. You will rise to an elevation of understanding with your wonderful guides. Send negative thoughts away by thought! – think only about beautifully things.

And while you are concentrating and losing yourself in the depth of that concentrative object, you will drift and you will immerse yourself completely out of the picture of materiality and all that beautiful medicine of God will come into your mind and body. Your guides will be there standing on your right and left side protecting your heart, lungs and your breathing, there is no fear because you have passed all danger zones. This is the outcome of the Law of Concentration. Your guides are well equipped with the knowledge of how to take care of you. You will have some wonderful excursions, when you are properly prepared for an astral flight. The aptitude of trance mediumship is good for your mind, body and self and gives you the ability to experience astral flight, to have a brief walk into the spirit world. The scene that you chose to focus your mind upon does not necessarily have to be of the material world. Think of something beautiful perhaps a loved one in spirit, smiling through Heaven's window at you or a flock of beautiful birds sailing high in the sky or the beautiful waters, peaceful, flowing with blueness, with seagulls circling above. Think of anything that is pleasing onto your senses. The greatest hindrance and the greatest stumbling block is when anyone allows their daily disappointments to get them down and keep them down. It is alright to fall down, once in a while but you must get up and rise, that's the ability of using the censoring powers of God.

Say to yourself: I am peace, I am love, I am faith, I am hope, I am charity, I love my Father God and love my angel love ones. I am a child of God; nothing can interfere with my progression.

Feel the tranquillity within you, the peace, love and understanding of the Law of Concentration. There is more in silence than in conversation".

~~~

Evening Séance 15/10/1989

Spirit Mabel Speaking:

"Children there will be days of discouragement, those are challenging days, those are the days when the old negatives draw closer to the physical plane, so call on the white light of Christ to surround you, these will not be penetrable. In the name of God, I say, may your vibrations be made higher and stronger! Try not to memorise everything you are told, I am not a teacher of the 'mimic law' and we don't want you to be a parrot taught person. We want you to be taught by actual
~~~

experience and we want the knowledge unveiled in your mind capsules. You have mind capsules ready to be filled. You will rejoice in seeing the revelations change day to day in your physical life and in your educational life.

It is wonderful to be here with you and it is wonderful to voice that from the heavenly world of God. When God sent His Son to the earth-plane, He dressed him in the form of mortal man, like man, because He wanted the world to know that within each person there is an identity of God, there is a personal identity of God in relationship of His own creation, so let us each day find ourselves further along the way of progression. That we might engage in spiritual and physical occupations so that you might call them a balance of life. God has a special way of shaping man's destiny; God gives unto man latent and wonderful talents. Sometimes it takes a long time to discover how blessed we really are. There are many times when you call things tragedies in life, often those tragedies reveal unto you how much you really have. It is sad to have them happen but when they do happen there is one remark I say, that sometimes they do awaken us to our consciousness.

Always abide by the laws of spirit – guard your temper – if any religion cannot do anything for your temper then it certainly cannot do anything for your soul – so temperament has a great role to play in mediumship. The annoyances that come like a thief in the night must be calmed. It is very knowable and very plausible and true that a worthy and capable person will be dragged down by negative forces. It exists universally with everything and everybody, without a competitive force there would be no progression. Neither would there be creation nor any innovations – innovation meaning newness. Try not to accept the negativity but be aware of its presence for you shall overcome it by the positive goodness that exists within you. This is the teachings of the Far East and the most high – that all positive goodness always supersedes negative existence. All negative existence goes in the smelting pot of destruction while all positive goodness rushes on into eternity and the flourishing blossoms of produce are the results of your steadfastness of faith and your endurance of patience and the overcoming of challenges. Therefore aware yourself and be on guard in the deepest moments of despair and disappointment. Use the superior mind of your own self, which is called super consciousness and fly from the naked pastures to the fields that are filled with beauty. Have faith, for faith is a substance, a substance of a belief in God and a substance which is evidential to God's manifestations".

~~~

Evening Séance 22/07/1989

Spirit Dr. Taylor Speaking:

"Hello Dr. Taylor here with you, adding to your education."

"Our religion is not one of speech alone it is one of action. It is of beauty and is one that as applicable meaning, it can be practiced in the everyday life of every person who lives in the physical plane or in another plane or dimension.
~~~

What is a medium? – a medium is an instrument between worlds – a medium is one who is sensitive to the vibrations of the spirit world and through whose instrumentality is able to convey messages back to the same, tuned into whatever height they are reaching, whether this be to the higher strata or the lower strata, depending on their thought form.

In the séance room when we refer to the definition of darkness as without light – we mean, without light is to be without understanding.

The three steps of Relaxation, Visualisation and Concentration are the keys to the advancement and unfoldment of mediumship. Relax the best that you can, by sitting in your chair correctly and in a comfortable position, be not tense in mind or body. The greatness of the spirit world and its power will come to you to work in the forms of mediumship – mental or physical. Those forms that are subjected to the mind and comprehended by the mind are classified as mental mediumship. Those that are comprehended and subjected by the physical are physical phenomena. The word phenomena are defined as 'something out of the ordinary'. When I put the 'a' at the end of phenomena it means the plural expression whereas phenomenon is the singular expression. So all phenomena are the units of all phases of mediumship, all those things that come out of the ordinary but yet they are natural. Not comprehended by the man of the physical world generally speaking because he who is a so-called scientist, none of his laws of science will prove the authenticity of phenomena or psychic happenings. It is impossible to explain psychic things by scientific methods of the physical world. This is because they must see them with the physical eye in its normal function or feel them with a physical touch in its normal function. They are without the use of extended vision or extended hearing. So in mediumship we go beyond the methods of the science of man.

Energy in the séance room is an influx, a surging power that comes in and out and from the centre core of divine intelligence which is God power. It is not how long you sit in the séance room but it is what happens while you sit in the energy – the blue mist of heaven. Patience is the virtue which is necessary for your unfoldment. Have conviction, be part of this and build your faith upon the rock of truth. Train yourself to be an able helper and enable yourself to be an instrument of God's peace.

Say this of yourselves: I am a child of God, I seek the still small voice of spirit, and may it call from me and out of me into the forestry of men, that they may find a blazing fire from the haunted woods of ignorance. May I find peace of mind, health of body and strength of action and find my God as I walk onward, one step at a time, always forward, always upwards. The pathways of the earth plane are cruel and rugged at times but if I fall face and when I am down, I will always look up or within.

Wisdom – the great doorway to happiness.

Love, health and happiness are the component parts of wisdom like the supernal triad – which comes from the extraction of the word superb – meaning the highest point of reach and the supernal triad – The Father, The Son and The Holy Spirit. Let this come into your life, knowing that God is in three parts. With those supernal parts you have nothing in life to fear. So use these valuable assets to open doors to the triangle of life. This triangle becomes the key to every door of success, of happiness, health and love. It opens the door to understanding and development. Your sincerity is guarded by one sentinel and that is yourself. You are the guardsman, the gatekeeper of your own wisdom. We can give wisdom to you but only you can take and treasure it. Only you can use and value it.

Metaphysical is a hard word to define. Metaphysics for everyday living will only be good, as long as it is attuned to the Godhead. The Godhead is the Holy Master of Order. The word infinite intelligence is the word that has often been use to express God. We believe in infinite intelligence and affirm that a correct understanding of such expression and living in accordance therewith, constitutes true religion. Infinite intelligence means God.

Words can be broken down in lifeless speech but trust lives in the heart forever. A man of his word is generally a businessman of the physical world, but a man of truth and trust lives on in the continuity of life. Trust yourself, trust your spirit guides but above all trust God in your mediumship. Out of pieces of ore come the greatest diamonds in the world. Let your mediumship shine through you as bright as any diamond".

Dear student – this concludes the spiritual work of James Garfield Tingley and John C Lilek. It is only a summary of their lengthy time of their workings with the spirit world and inhabitants. But even in the small amount documented, it is hoped you acknowledge their vocation and contributions to the religion of mediumship. It is hoped too that you find inspiration for your own mediumship and aspire to become a true, steadfast, honest servant of God and spirit.

Let your mediumship shine through and its radiance will attract the highest and the brightest of spirits. Be worthy to hold the title of Medium for you are carrying our Heritage, which must be passed on as being perfect. May spirit love and guidance be ever with you on your unfolding journey of life with spirit!
K.M.

"We do not see physic science as a hobby it is the study of the soul world, the spiritual world of continuance. We do not regard the physical plane as other than the beginning or the ending of life, it is just one of the stop offs."

Quote from spirit of Arthur C Doyle during J G Tingley séance – 1989.